POEMS.

Oliver Wendell Holmes

POEMS

BY

OLIVER WENDELL HOLMES.

NEW AND ENLARGED EDITION.

BOSTON:
TICKNOR AND FIELDS.
M DCCC LVI.

Damrell & Moore, Printers, Boston.

THE AUTHOR TO THE PUBLISHERS.

I THANK you for the pains you have taken to bring together the poems now added to this collection; one of them having been accidentally omitted, and the existence of the others forgotten. So many productions which bear the plain marks of immaturity and inexperience have been allowed to remain, because they were in the earlier editions, that a few occasional and careless stanzas may be added to their company without any apology. I have no doubt you are right in thinking that there is no harm in allowing a few crudities to keep their place among the rest; for, as you suggest, the readers of a book are of various ages and tastes, and what sounds altogether schoolboy-like to the author may be very author-like to the schoolboy. Some of the more questionable extravagances to be found in the earlier portion of the volume, have, as I learn, pleased a good many young people; let us call these, and all the others that we have outgrown, *Juvenile Poems*, but keep them, lest some of the smaller sort that were, or are, or are to be, should lament their absence. I thought of mentioning the date at which the several poems were written, which would explain some of their differences; but the reader can judge them nearly enough, perhaps, without this assistance.

To save a question that is sometimes put, it is proper to say that in naming two of the poems after two of the Muses, nothing more was intended than a suggestion of their general character and aim. In a former note of mine (which you printed as a kind of preface to the last edition), I made certain explanations which I thought might be needed; but as nobody seems to have misinterpreted any thing, we will trust our book hereafter to itself, not doubting that whatever is good in it will redeem and justify the rest.

Boston, January 13th, 1849.

CONTENTS.

LYRICS.

TO

CHARLES WENTWORTH UPHAM

THE FOLLOWING

METRICAL ESSAY

IS AFFECTIONATELY INSCRIBED.

POETRY;

A METRICAL ESSAY.

Scenes of my youth![1] awake its slumbering fire!
Ye winds of Memory, sweep the silent lyre!
Ray of the past, if yet thou canst appear,
Break through the clouds of Fancy's waning year;
Chase from her breast the thin autumnal snow,
If leaf or blossom still is fresh below!

Long have I wandered ; the returning tide
Brought back an exile to his cradle's side ;
And as my bark her time-worn flag unrolled,
To greet the land-breeze with its faded fold,
So, in remembrance of my boyhood's time,
I lift these ensigns of neglected rhyme ; —
O more than blest, that, all my wanderings through,
My anchor falls where first my pennons flew !

The morning light, which rains its quivering beams
Wide o'er the plains, the summits, and the streams,
In one broad blaze expands its golden glow
On all that answers to its glance below ;
Yet, changed on earth, each far reflected ray
Braids with fresh hues the shining brow of day ;
Now, clothed in blushes by the painted flowers,
Tracks on their cheeks the rosy-fingered hours ;
Now, lost in shades, whose dark entangled leaves
Drip at the noontide from their pendent eaves,
Fades into gloom, or gleams in light again
From every dew-drop on the jewelled plain.

We, like the leaf, the summit, or the wave,
Reflect the light our common nature gave,
But every sunbeam, falling from her throne,
Wears, on our hearts, some coloring of our own;
Chilled in the slave, and burning in the free,
Like the sealed cavern by the sparkling sea;
Lost, like the lightning in the sullen clod,
Or shedding radiance, like the smiles of God,
Pure, pale in Virtue, as the star above,
Or quivering roseate on the leaves of Love;
Glaring like noontide, where it glows upon
Ambition's sands, — the desert in the sun;
Or soft suffusing o'er the varied scene
Life's common coloring, — intellectual green.

Thus Heaven, repeating its material plan,
Arched over all the rainbow mind of man;
But he, who, blind to universal laws,
Sees but effects, unconscious of their cause, —
Believes each image in itself is bright,
Not robed in drapery of reflected light, —
Is like the rustic, who, amidst his toil,
Has found some crystal in his meagre soil,
And, lost in rapture, thinks for him alone
Earth worked her wonders on the sparkling stone,

Nor dreams that Nature, with as nice a line,
Carved countless angles through the boundless mine.

Thus err the many, who, entranced to find
Unwonted lustre in some clearer mind,
Believe that Genius sets the laws at nought
Which chain the pinions of our wildest thought;
Untaught to measure, with the eye of art,
The wandering fancy or the wayward heart;
Who match the little only with the less,
And gaze in rapture at its slight excess,
Proud of a pebble, as the brightest gem
Whose light might crown an emperor's diadem.

And, most of all, the pure ethereal fire,
Which seems to radiate from the poet's lyre,
Is to the world a mystery and a charm,
An Ægis wielded on a mortal's arm,
While Reason turns her dazzled eye away,
And bows her sceptre to her subject's sway;
And thus the poet, clothed with godlike state
Usurped his Maker's title — to create;
He, whose thoughts differing not in shape, but dress,
What others feel, more fitly can express,
Sits like the maniac on his fancied throne,
Peeps through the bars, and calls the world his own.

There breathes no being but has some pretence
To that fine instinct called poetic sense;
The rudest savage roaming through the wild,
The simplest rustic, bending o'er his child,
The infant listening to the warbling bird,
The mother smiling at its half-formed word;
The boy uncaged, who tracks the fields at large,
The girl, turned matron to her babe-like charge;
The freeman, casting with unpurchased hand
The vote that shakes the turrets of the land;
The slave, who, slumbering on his rusted chain,
Dreams of the palm-trees on his burning plain;
The hot-cheeked reveller, tossing down the wine,
To join the chorus pealing "Auld lang syne";
The gentle maid, whose azure eye grows dim,
While Heaven is listening to her evening hymn;
The jewelled beauty, when her steps draw near
The circling dance and dazzling chandelier;
E'en trembling age, when Spring's renewing air
Waves the thin ringlets of his silvered hair; —
All, all are glowing with the inward flame,
Whose wider halo wreaths the poet's name,
While, unembalmed, the silent dreamer dies,
His memory passing with his smiles and sighs!

If glorious visions, born for all mankind,
The bright auroras of our twilight mind;
If fancies, varying as the shapes that lie
Stained on the windows of the sunset sky;
If hopes, that beckon with delusive gleams,
Till the eye dances in the void of dreams;
If passions, following with the winds that urge
Earth's wildest wanderer to her farthest verge;—
If these on all some transient hours bestow
Of rapture tingling with its hectic glow,
Then all are poets; and, if earth had rolled
Her myriad centuries, and her doom were told,
Each moaning billow of her shoreless wave
Would wail its requiem o'er a poet's grave!

If to embody in a breathing word
Tones that the spirit trembled when it heard·
To fix the image all unveiled and warm,
And carve in language its ethereal form,
So pure, so perfect, that the lines express
No meagre shrinking, no unlaced excess;
To feel that art, in living truth, has taught
Ourselves, reflected in the sculptured thought;—
If this alone bestow the right to claim
The deathless garland and the sacred name;

Then none are poets, save the saints on high,
Whose harps can murmur all that words deny!

But though to none is granted to reveal,
In perfect semblance, all that each may feel,
As withered flowers recall forgotten love,
So, warmed to life, our faded passions move
In every line, where kindling fancy throws
The gleam of pleasures, or the shade of woes.

When, schooled by time, the stately queen of art
Had smoothed the pathways leading to the heart,
Assumed her measured tread, her solemn tone,
And round her courts the clouds of fable thrown,
The wreaths of heaven descended on her shrine,
And wondering earth proclaimed the Muse divine
Yet, if her votaries had but dared profane
The mystic symbols of her sacred reign,
How had they smiled beneath the veil to find
What slender threads can chain the mighty mind

Poets, like painters, their machinery claim,
And verse bestows the varnish and the frame;
Our grating English, whose Teutonic jar
Shakes the racked axle of Art's rattling car,

Fits like mosaic in the lines that gird
Fast in its place each many-angled word;
From Saxon lips Anacreon's numbers glide,
As once they melted on the Teian tide,
And, fresh transfused, the Iliad thrills again
From Albion's cliffs as o'er Achaia's plain!
The proud heroic, with its pulse-like beat,
Rings like the cymbals clashing as they meet;
The sweet Spenserian, gathering as it flows,
Sweeps gently onward to its dying close,
Where waves on waves in long succession pour,
Till the ninth billow melts along the shore;
The lonely spirit of the mournful lay,
Which lives immortal as the verse of Gray,
In sable plumage slowly drifts along,
On eagle pinion, through the air of song;
The glittering lyric bounds elastic by,
With flashing ringlets and exulting eye,
While every image, in her airy whirl,
Gleams like a diamond on a dancing girl![2]

Born with mankind, with man's expanded range
And varying fates the poet's numbers change;
Thus in his history may we hope to find
Some clearer epochs of the poet's mind,

As from the cradle of its birth we trace,
Slow wandering forth, the patriarchal race.

I.

When the green earth, beneath the zephyr's wing,
Wears on her breast the varnished buds of Spring;
When the loosed current, as its folds uncoil,
Slides in the channels of the mellowed soil;
When the young hyacinth returns to seek
The air and sunshine with her emerald beak;
When the light snowdrops, starting from their cells,
Hang each pagoda with its silver bells;
When the frail willow twines her trailing bow
With pallid leaves that sweep the soil below;
When the broad elm, sole empress of the plain,
Whose circling shadow speaks a century's reign,
Wreaths in the clouds her regal diadem,—
A forest waving on a single stem;—
Then mark the poet; though to him unknown
The quaint-mouthed titles, such as scholars own,
See how his eye in ecstasy pursues
The steps of Nature tracked in radiant hues;
Nay, in thyself, whate'er may be thy fate,
Pallid with toil, or surfeited with state,

Maik how thy fancies, with the vernal rose,
Awake, all sweetness, from their long repose;
Then turn to ponder o'er the classic page,
Traced with the idyls of a greener age,
And learn the instinct which arose to warm
Art's earliest essay, and her simplest form.

To themes like these her narrow path confined
The first-born impulse moving in the mind;
In vales unshaken by the trumpet's sound,
Where peaceful Labor tills his fertile ground,
The silent changes of the rolling years,
Marked on the soil, or dialled on the spheres,
The crested forests and the colored flowers,
The dewy grottos and the blushing bowers,
These, and their guardians, who, with liquid names,
Strephons and Chloes, melt in mutual flames,
Woo the young Muses from their mountain shade,
To make Arcadias in the lonely glade.

Nor think they visit only with their smiles
The fabled valleys and Elysian isles;
He who is wearied of his village plain
May roam the Edens of the world in vain.
'T is not the star-crowned cliff, the cataract's flow,
The softer foliage, or the greener glow,

The lake of sapphire, or the spar-hung cave,
The brighter sunset, or the broader wave,
Can warm his heart whom every wind has blown
To every shore, forgetful of his own.

Home of our childhood! how affection clings
And hovers round thee with her seraph wings!
Dearer thy hills, though clad in autumn brown,
Than fairest summits which the cedars crown!
Sweeter the fragrance of thy summer breeze
Than all Arabia breathes along the seas!
The stranger's gale wafts home the exile's sigh,
For the heart's temple is its own blue sky!

O happiest they, whose early love unchanged,
Hopes undissolved, and friendship unestranged,
Tired of their wanderings, still can deign to see
Love, hopes, and friendship, centering all in thee!

And thou, my village! as again I tread
Amidst thy living, and above thy dead;
Though some fair playmates guard with chaster fears
Their cheeks, grown holy with the lapse of years;
Though with the dust some reverend locks may blend,
Where life's last mile-stone marks the journey's end;

On every bud the changing year recalls,
The brightening glance of morning memory falls,
Still following onward as the months unclose
The balmy lilac or the bridal rose ;
And still shall follow, till they sink once more
Beneath the snow-drifts of the frozen shore,
As when my bark, long tossing in the gale,
Furled in her port her tempest-rended sail !

What shall I give thee ? Can a simple lay,
Flung on thy bosom like a girl's bouquet,
Do more than deck thee for an idle hour,
Then fall unheeded, fading like the flower ?
Yet, when I trod, with footsteps wild and free,
The crackling leaves beneath yon linden tree,
Panting from play, or dripping from the stream,
How bright the visions of my boyish dream !
Or, modest Charles, along thy broken edge,
Black with soft ooze and fringed with arrowy sedge,
As once I wandered in the morning sun,
With reeking sandal and superfluous gun ;
How oft, as Fancy whispered in the gale,
Thou wast the Avon of her flattering tale !
Ye hills, whose foliage, fretted on the skies,
Prints shadowy arches on their evening dyes,

How should my song, with holiest charm, invest
Each dark ravine and forest-lifting crest!
How clothe in beauty each familiar scene,
Till all was classic on my native green!

As the drained fountain, filled with autumn leaves,
The field swept naked of its garnered sheaves;
So wastes at noon the promise of our dawn,
The springs all choking, and the harvest gone.

Yet hear the lay of one whose natal star
Still seemed the brightest when it shone afar;
Whose cheek, grown pallid with ungracious toil,
Glows in the welcome of his parent soil;
And ask no garlands sought beyond the tide,
But take the leaflets gathered at your side.

Our ancient church! its lowly tower,
Beneath the loftier spire,
Is shadowed when the sunset hour
Clothes the tall shaft in fire;
It sinks beyond the distant eye,
Long ere the glittering vane,
High wheeling in the western sky,
Has faded o'er the plain.

Like Sentinel and Nun, they keep
    Their vigil on the green;
One seems to guard, and one to weep,
    The dead that lie between;
And both roll out, so full and near,
    Their music's mingling waves,
They shake the grass, whose pennoned spear
    Leans on the narrow graves.

The stranger parts the flaunting weeds,
    Whose seeds the winds have strown
So thick beneath the line he reads,
    They shade the sculptured stone;
The child unveils his clustered brow,
    And ponders for a while
The graven willow's pendent bough,
    Or rudest cherub's smile.

But what to them the dirge, the knell?
    These were the mourner's share;—
The sullen clang, whose heavy swell
    Throbbed through the beating air;—
The rattling cord,—the rolling stone,—
    The shelving sand that slid,
And, far beneath, with hollow tone,
    Rung on the coffin's lid.

The slumberer's mound grows fresh and green,
Then slowly disappears;
The mosses creep, the gray stones lean,
Earth hides his date and years;
But, long before the once-loved name
Is sunk or worn away,
No lip the silent dust may claim,
That pressed the breathing clay.

Go where the ancient pathway guides,
See where our sires laid down
Their smiling babes, their cherished brides,
The patriarchs of the town;
Hast thou a tear for buried love?
A sigh for transient power?
All that a century left above,
Go, read it in an hour!

The Indian's shaft, the Briton's ball,
The sabre's thirsting edge,
The hot shell, shattering in its fall,
The bayonet's rending wedge, —
Here scattered death; yet, seek the spot,
No trace thine eye can see,
No altar, — and they need it not
Who leave their children free!

Look where the turbid rain-drops stand
    In many a chiselled square,
The knightly crest, the shield, the brand
    Of honored names were there, —
Alas! for every tear is dried
    Those blazoned tablets knew,
Save when the icy marble's side
    Drips with the evening dew.

Or gaze upon yon pillared stone,[3]
    The empty urn of pride;
There stand the Goblet and the Sun, —
    What need of more beside?
Where lives the memory of the dead,
    Who made their tomb a toy?
Whose ashes press that nameless bed?
    Go, ask the village boy!

Lean o'er the slender western wall,
    Ye ever-roaming girls;
The breath that bids the blossom fall
    May lift your floating curls,
To sweep the simple lines that tell
    An exile's date and doom;
And sigh, for where his daughters dwell,
    They wreath the stranger's tomb.

And one amid these shades was born,
    Beneath this turf who lies,
Once beaming as the summer's morn,
    That closed her gentle eyes ; —
If sinless angels love as we,
    Who stood thy grave beside,
Three seraph welcomes waited thee,
    The daughter, sister, bride !

I wandered to thy buried mound
    When earth was hid below
The level of the glaring ground,
    Choked to its gates with snow,
And when with summer's flowery waves
    The lake of verdure rolled,
As if a Sultan's white-robed slaves
    Had scattered pearls and gold.

Nay, the soft pinions of the air,
    That lift this trembling tone,
Its breath of love may almost bear,
    To kiss thy funeral stone ; —
And, now thy smiles have passed away,
    For all the joy they gave,
May sweetest dews and warmest ray
    Lie on thine early grave !

When damps beneath, and storms above,
  Have bowed these fragile towers,
Still o'er the graves yon locust-grove
  Shall swing its Orient flowers;—
And I would ask no mouldering bust,
  If e'er this humble line,
Which breathed a sigh o'er other's dust,
  Might call a tear on mine.

II.

But times were changed; the torch of terror came,
To light the summits with the beacon's flame;
The streams ran crimson, the tall mountain pines
Rose a new forest o'er embattled lines;
The bloodless sickle lent the warrior's steel,
The harvest bowed beneath his chariot wheel;
Where late the wood-dove sheltered her repose,
The raven waited for the conflict's close;
The cuirassed sentry walked his sleepless round
Where Daphne smiled or Amaryllis frowned;
Where timid minstrels sung their blushing charms,
Some wild Tyrtæus called aloud, "To arms!"

When Glory wakes, when fiery spirits leap,
Roused by her accents from their tranquil sleep,
The ray that flashes from the soldier's crest,
Lights, as it glances, in the poet's breast;—
Not in pale dreamers, whose fantastic lay
Toys with smooth trifles like a child at play,
But men, who act the passions they inspire,
Who wave the sabre as they sweep the lyre!

Ye mild enthusiasts, whose pacific frowns
Are lost like dew-drops caught in burning towns,
Pluck as ye will the radiant plumes of fame,
Break Cæsar's bust to make yourselves a name,
But, if your country bares the avenger's blade
For wrongs unpunished, or for debts unpaid,
When the roused nation bids her armies form,
And screams her eagle through the gathering storm
When from your ports the bannered frigate rides,
Her black bows scowling to the crested tides,
Your hour has past; in vain your feeble cry,
As the babe's wailings to the thundering sky!

Scourge of mankind! with all the dread array,
That wraps in wrath thy desolating way,
As the wild tempest wakes the slumbering sea,
Thou only teachest all that man can be.

Alike thy tocsin has the power to charm
The toil-knit sinews of the rustic's arm,
Or swell the pulses in the poet's veins,
And bid the nations tremble at his strains.

The city slept beneath the moonbeam's glance,
Her white walls gleaming through the vines of France,
And all was hushed, save where the footsteps fell,
On some high tower, of midnight sentinel.
But one still watched; no self-encircled woes
Chased from his lids the angel of repose;
He watched, he wept, for thoughts of bitter years
Bowed his dark lashes, wet with burning tears;
His country's sufferings and her children's shame
Streamed o'er his memory like a forest's flame,
Each treasured insult, each remembered wrong,
Rolled through his heart and kindled into song;
His taper faded; and the morning gales
Swept through the world the war-song of Marseilles![4]

Now, while around the smiles of Peace expand,
And Plenty's wreaths festoon the laughing land;
While France ships outward her reluctant ore,
And half our navy basks upon the shore;
From ruder themes our meek-eyed Muses turn
To crown with roses their enamelled urn.

If e'er again return those awful days
Whose clouds were crimsoned with the beacon's blaze,
Whose grass was trampled by the soldier's heel,
Whose tides were reddened round the rushing keel,
God grant some lyre may wake a nobler strain,
To rend the silence of our tented plain!
When Gallia's flag its triple fold displays,
Her marshalled legions peal the Marseillaise;
When round the German close the war-clouds dim,
Far through their shadows floats his battle-hymn;
When, crowned with joy, the camps of England ring,
A thousand voices shout, "God save the King!"
When victory follows with our eagle's glance,
Our nation's anthem is a country dance![5]

Some prouder muse, when comes the hour at last,
May shake our hill-sides with her bugle-blast;
Not ours the task; but since the lyric dress
Relieves the statelier with its sprightliness,
Hear an old song, which some, perchance, have seen
In stale gazette, or cobwebbed magazine.
There was an hour when patriots dared profane
The mast that Britain strove to bow in vain;[6]
And one, who listened to the tale of shame,
Whose heart still answered to that sacred name,

Whose eye still followed o'er his country's tides
Thy glorious flag, our brave Old Ironsides!
From yon lone attic, on a summer's morn,
Thus mocked the spoilers with his school-boy scorn.

Ay, tear her tattered ensign down!
Long has it waved on high,
And many an eye has danced to see
That banner in the sky;
Beneath it rung the battle shout,
And burst the cannon's roar;—
The meteor of the ocean air
Shall sweep the clouds no more!

Her deck, once red with heroes' blood,
Where knelt the vanquished foe,
When winds were hurrying o'er the flood,
And waves were white below,
No more shall feel the victor's tread,
Or know the conquered knee;—
The harpies of the shore shall pluck
The eagle of the sea!

O better that her shattered hulk
Should sink beneath the wave;
Her thunders shook the mighty deep,
And there should be her grave;
Nail to the mast her holy flag,
Set every threadbare sail,
And give her to the god of storms,
The lightning and the gale!

III.

When florid Peace resumed her golden reign,
And arts revived, and valleys bloomed again;
While War still panted on his broken blade,
Once more the Muse her heavenly wing essayed.
Rude was the song; some ballad, stern and wild,
Lulled the light slumbers of the soldier's child;
Or young romancer with his threatening glance
And fearful fables of his bloodless lance,
Scared the soft fancy of the clinging girls,
Whose snowy fingers smoothed his raven curls.
But when long years the stately form had bent,
And faithless memory her illusions lent,

So vast the outlines of Tradition grew,
That History wondered at the shapes she drew,
And veiled at length their too ambitious hues
Beneath the pinions of the Epic Muse.

Far swept her wing; for stormier days had brought
With darker passions deeper tides of thought.
The camp's harsh tumult and the conflict's glow,
The thrill of triumph and the gasp of woe,
The tender parting and the glad return,
The festal banquet and the funeral urn, —
And all the drama which at once uprears
Its spectral shadows through the clash of spears,
From camp and field to echoing verse transferred,
Swelled the proud song that listening nations heard.

Why floats the amaranth in eternal bloom
O'er Ilium's turrets and Achilles' tomb?
Why lingers fancy, where the sunbeams smile
On Circe's gardens and Calypso's isle?
Why follows memory to the gate of Troy
Her plumed defender and his trembling boy?
Lo the blind dreamer, kneeling on the sand,
To trace these records with his doubtful hand;

In fabled tones his own emotion flows,
And other lips repeat his silent woes;
In Hector's infant see the babes that shun
Those deathlike eyes, unconscious of the sun,
Or in his hero hear himself implore,
"Give me to see, and Ajax asks no more!"

Thus live undying through the lapse of time
The solemn legends of the warrior's clime;
Like Egypt's pyramid, or Pæstum's fane,
They stand the heralds of the voiceless plain;
Yet not like them, for Time, by slow degrees,
Saps the gray stone, and wears the chiselled frieze,
And Isis sleeps beneath her subject Nile,
And crumbled Neptune strews his Dorian pile;
But Art's fair fabric, strengthening as it rears
Its laurelled columns through the mist of years,
As the blue arches of the bending skies
Still gird the torrent, following as it flies,
Spreads, with the surges bearing on mankind,
Its starred pavilion o'er the tides of mind!

In vain the patriot asks some lofty lay
To dress in state our wars of yesterday.
The classic days, those mothers of romance,
That roused a nation for a woman's glance;

The age of mystery with its hoarded power,
That girt the tyrant in his storied tower,
Have past and faded like a dream of youth,
And riper eras ask for history's truth.

On other shores, above their mouldering towns,
In sullen pomp the tall cathedral frowns,
Pride in its aisles, and paupers at the door,
Which feeds the beggars whom it fleeced of yore.
Simple and frail, our lowly temples throw
Their slender shadows on the paths below;
Scarce steal the winds, that sweep his woodland tracks,
The larch's perfume from the settler's axe,
Ere, like a vision of the morning air,
His slight-framed steeple marks the house of prayer;
Its planks all reeking, and its paint undried,
Its rafters sprouting on the shady side,
It sheds the raindrops from its shingled eaves,
Ere its green brothers once have changed their leaves.

Yet Faith's pure hymn, beneath its shelter rude,
Breathes out as sweetly to the tangled wood,
As where the rays through blazing oriels pour
On marble shaft and tessellated floor;—
Heaven asks no surplice round the heart that feels,
And all is holy where devotion kneels.

Thus on the soil the patriot's knee should bend,
Which holds the dust once living to defend;
Where'er the hireling shrinks before the free,
Each pass becomes "a new Thermopylæ"!
Where'er the battles of the brave are won,
There every mountain "looks on Marathon"!

Our fathers live; they guard in glory still
The grass-grown bastions of the fortressed hill;
Still ring the echoes of the trampled gorge,
With *God and Freedom! England and Saint George*.
The royal cipher on the captured gun
Mocks the sharp night-dews and the blistering sun!
The red-cross banner shades its captor's bust,
Its folds still loaded with the conflict's dust;
The drum, suspended by its tattered marge,
Once rolled and rattled to the Hessian's charge;
The stars have floated from Britannia's mast,
The redcoat's trumpets blown the rebel's blast.

Point to the summits where the brave have bled,
Where every village claims its glorious dead;
Say, when their bosoms met the bayonet's shock,
Their only corslet was the rustic frock;
Say, when they mustered to the gathering horn,
The titled chieftain curled his lip in scorn,

Yet, when their leader bade his lines advance
No musket wavered in the lion's glance;
Say, when they fainted in the forced retreat,
They tracked the snow-drifts with their bleeding feet,
Yet still their banners, tossing in the blast,
Bore *Ever Ready*,[7] faithful to the last,
Through storm and battle, till they waved again
On Yorktown's hills and Saratoga's plain!

Then, if so fierce the insatiate patriot's flame,
Truth looks too pale, and history seems too tame,
Bid him await some new Columbiad's page,
To gild the tablets of an iron age,
And save his tears, which yet may fall upon
Some fabled field, some fancied Washington!

IV.

But once again, from their Æolian cave,
The winds of Genius wandered on the wave.
Tired of the scenes the timid pencil drew,
Sick of the notes the sounding clarion blew;
Sated with heroes who had worn so long
The shadowy plumage of historic song;
The new-born poet left the beaten course,
To track the passions to their living source.

Then rose the Drama ; — and the world admired
Her varied page with deeper thought inspired ;
Bound to no clime, for Passion's throb is one
In Greenland's twilight or in India's sun ;
Born for no age, — for all the thoughts that roll
In the dark vortex of the stormy soul,
Unchained in song, no freezing years can tame ;
God gave them birth, and man is still the same.

So full on life her magic mirror shone,
Her sister Arts paid tribute to her throne ;
One reared her temple, one her canvass warmed,
And Music thrilled, while Eloquence informed.
The weary rustic left his stinted task
For smiles and tears, the dagger and the mask ;
The sage, turned scholar, half forgot his lore,
To be the woman he despised before ;
O'er sense and thought she threw her golden chain,
And Time, the anarch, spares her deathless reign.

Thus lives Medea, in our tamer age,
As when her buskin pressed the Grecian stage ;
Not in the cells where frigid learning delves
In Aldine folios mouldering on their shelves ;
But breathing, burning in the glittering throng,
Whose thousand bravos roll untired along,

Circling and spreading through the gilded halls,
From London's galleries to San Carlo's walls!

Thus shall he live whose more than mortal name
Mocks with its ray the pallid torch of Fame;
So proudly lifted, that it seems afar
No earthly Pharos, but a heavenly star;
Who, unconfined to Art's diurnal bound,
Girds her whole zodiac in his flaming round,
And leads the passions, like the orb that guides,
From pole to pole, the palpitating tides!

V.

Though round the Muse the robe of song is thrown,
Think not the poet lives in verse alone.
Long ere the chisel of the sculptor taught
The lifeless stone to mock the living thought;
Long ere the painter bade the canvass glow
With every line the forms of beauty know;
Long ere the Iris of the Muses threw
On every leaf its own celestial hue;
In fable's dress the breath of genius poured,
And warmed the shapes that later times adored.

Untaught by Science how to forge the keys,
That loose the gates of Nature's mysteries;
Unschooled by Faith, who, with her angel tread,
Leads through the labyrinth with a single thread,
His fancy, hovering round her guarded tower,
Rained through its bars like Danae's golden shower.

He spoke; the sea-nymph answered from her cave:
He called; the naiad left her mountain wave:
He dreamed of beauty; lo, amidst his dream,
Narcissus mirrored in the breathless stream;
And night's chaste empress, in her bridal play,
Laughed through the foliage where Endymion lay;
And ocean dimpled, as the languid swell
Kissed the red lip of Cytherea's shell:
Of power,—Bellona swept the crimson field,
And blue-eyed Pallas shook her Gorgon shield;
O'er the hushed waves their mightier monarch drove
And Ida trembled to the tread of Jove!

So every grace, that plastic language knows,
To nameless poets its perfection owes.
The rough-hewn words to simplest thoughts confined,
Were cut and polished in their nicer mind;
Caught on their edge, imagination's ray
Splits into rainbows, shooting far away;—

From sense to soul, from soul to sense, it flies,
And through all nature links analogies;
He who reads right will rarely look upon
A better poet than his lexicon!

There is a race, which cold, ungenial skies
Breed from decay, as fungous growths arise;
Though dying fast, yet springing fast again,
Which still usurps an unsubstantial reign.
With frames too languid for the charms of sense,
And minds worn down with action too intense;
Tired of a world whose joys they never knew,
Themselves deceived, yet thinking all untrue;
Scarce men without. and less than girls within.
Sick of their life before its cares begin;—
The dull disease, which drains their feeble hearts,
To life's decay some hectic thrills imparts,
And lends a force, which, like the maniac's power,
Pays with blank years the frenzy of an hour.

And this is Genius! Say, does Heaven degrade
The manly frame, for health, for action made?
Break down the sinews, rack the brow with pains,
Blanch the bright cheek, and drain the purple veins,
To clothe the mind with more extended sway,
Thus faintly struggling in degenerate clay?

No! gentle maid, too ready to admire,
Though false its notes, the pale enthusiast's lyre;
If this be genius, though its bitter springs
Glowed like the morn beneath Aurora's wings,
Seek not the source whose sullen bosom feeds
But fruitless flowers, and dark, envenomed weeds.

But, if so bright the dear illusion seems,
Thou wouldst be partner of thy poet's dreams,
And hang in rapture on his bloodless charms,
Or die, like Raphael, in his angel arms;
Go, and enjoy thy blessed lot, — to share
In Cowper's gloom, or Chatterton's despair!

Not such were they, whom, wandering o'er the waves,
I looked to meet, but only found their graves;
If friendship's smile, the better part of fame,
Should lend my song the only wreath I claim,
Whose voice would greet me with a sweeter tone,
Whose living hand more kindly press my own,
Than theirs, — could Memory, as her silent tread
Prints the pale flowers that blossom o'er the dead,
Those breathless lips, now closed in peace, restore,
Or wake those pulses hushed to beat no more?

Thou calm, chaste scholar![8] I can see thee now,
The first young laurels on thy pallid brow,
O'er thy slight figure floating lightly down
In graceful folds the academic gown,
On thy curled lip the classic lines, that taught
How nice the mind that sculptured them with thought,
And triumph glistening in the clear blue eye,
Too bright to live, — but oh, too fair to die!

And thou, dear friend,[9] whom Science still deplores
And love still mourns, on ocean-severed shores,
Though the bleak forest twice has bowed with snow,
Since thou wast laid its budding leaves below,
Thine image mingles with my closing strain,
As when we wandered by the turbid Seine,
Both blest with hopes, which revelled, bright and free,
On all we longed, or all we dreamed to be;
To thee the amaranth and the cypress fell, —
And I was spared to breathe this last farewell!

But lived there one in unremembered days,
Or lives there still, who spurns the poet's bays?
Whose fingers, dewy from Castalia's springs,
Rest on the lyre, yet scorn to touch the strings?

Who shakes the senate with the silver tone
The groves of Pindus might have sighed to own?
Have such e'er been? Remember Canning's name!
Do such still live? Let "Alaric's Dirge" proclaim!

Immortal Art! where'er the rounded sky
Bends o'er the cradle where thy children lie,
Their home is earth, their herald every tongue
Whose accents echo to the voice that sung.
One leap of Ocean scatters on the sand
The quarried bulwarks of the loosening land;
One thrill of earth dissolves a century's toil,
Strewed like the leaves that vanish in the soil;
One hill o'erflows, and cities sink below,
Their marbles splintering in the lava's glow;
But one sweet tone, scarce whispered to the air,
From shore to shore the blasts of ages bear;
One humble name, which oft, perchance, has borne
The tyrant's mockery and the courtier's scorn,
Towers o'er the dust of earth's forgotten graves,
As once, emerging through the waste of waves,
The rocky Titan, round whose shattered spear
Coiled the last whirlpool of the drowning sphere!

NOTES.

Note 1. Page 1.

" *Scenes of my youth.*"

This poem was commenced a few months subsequently to the author's return to his native village, after an absence of nearly three years.

Note 2. Page 8.

A few lines, perhaps deficient in dignity, were introduced at this point, in delivering the poem, and are appended in this clandestine manner for the gratification of some of my audience.

How many a stanza, blushing like the rose,
Would turn to fustian if resolved to prose!
How many an epic, like a gilded crown,
If some cold critic dared to melt it down,
Roll in his crucible a shapeless mass,
A grain of gold-leaf to a pound of brass!
Shorn of their plumes, our moonstruck sonneteers
Would seem but jackdaws croaking to the spheres;

Our gay Lotharios, with their Byron curls,
Would pine like oysters cheated of their pearls!

Wo to the spectres of Parnassus' shade,
If truth should mingle in the masquerade.
Lo, as the songster's pale creations pass,
Off come at once the "Dearest" and "Alas!"
Crack go the lines and levers used to prop
Top-heavy thoughts, and down at once they drop.
Flowers weep for *hours; Love*, shrieking for his *dove*,
Finds not the solace that he seeks — above.
Fast in the mire, through which in happier time
He ambled dryshod on the stilts of rhyme,
The prostrate poet finds at length a tongue
To curse in prose the thankless stars he sung.

And though, perchance, the haughty muse it shames
How deep the magic of harmonious names!
How sure the story of romance to please,
Whose rounded stanza ends with Heloise!
How rich and full our intonations ride
"On Torno's cliffs, or Pambamarca's side"!
But were her name some vulgar "proper noun,"
And Pambamarca changed to Belchertown,
She might be pilloried for her doubtful fame,
And no enthusiast would arise to blame;
And he who outraged the poetic sense,
Might find a home at Belchertown's expense!

The harmless boys, scarce knowing right from wrong,
Who libel others and themselves in song.
When their first pothooks of poetic rage
Slant down the corners of an album's page,
(Where crippled couplets spread their sprawling charms,
As half-taught swimmers move their legs and arms,)
Will talk of "Hesper on the brow of eve,"
And call their cousins "lovely Genevieve"; —
While thus transformed, each dear deluded maid,
Pleased with herself in novel grace arrayed,
Smiles on the Paris who has come to crown
This newborn Helen in a gingham gown!

Note 3. Page 16.

"*Or gaze upon yon pillared stone.*"

The tomb of the VASSALL family is marked by a freestone tablet, supported by five pillars, and bearing nothing but the sculptured reliefs of the Goblet and the Sun, — *Vas-Sol* — which designated a powerful family, now almost forgotten.

The exile referred to in the next stanza was a native of Honfleur in Normandy.

Note 4. Page 20.

"*Swept through the world the war-song of Marseilles.*"

The music and words of the Marseilles Hymn were composed in one night.

Note 5. Page 21.

"*Our nation's anthem is a country dance!*"

The popular air of "Yankee Doodle," like the dagger of Hudibras, serves a pacific as well as a martial purpose.

Note 6. Page 21.

"*The mast that Britain strove to bow in vain.*"

The lyric which follows was printed in the "Boston Daily Advertiser," at the time when it was proposed to break up the frigate Constitution as unfit for service.

Note 7. Page 28.

"*Bore* Ever Ready, *faithful to the last.*"

"*Semper paratus,*"—a motto of the revolutionary standards.

Note 8. Page 34.

"*Thou calm, chaste scholar.*"

Charles Chauncy Emerson; died May 9th, 1836.

Note 9. Page 34.

"*And thou, dear friend.*"

James Jackson, Jr., M. D.; died March 29th, 1834.

LYRICS.

LYRICS.

THE LAST READER.

I sometimes sit beneath a tree,
And read my own sweet songs;
Though nought they may to others be,
Each humble line prolongs
A tone that might have passed away,
But for that scarce remembered lay.

I keep them like a lock or leaf,
That some dear girl has given;
Frail record of an hour, as brief
As sunset clouds in heaven,
But spreading purple twilight still
High over memory's shadowed hill.

They lie upon my pathway bleak,
Those flowers that once ran wild,
As on a father's care-worn cheek
The ringlets of his child;
The golden mingling with the gray,
And stealing half its snows away.

What care I though the dust is spread
Around these yellow leaves,
Or o'er them his sarcastic thread
Oblivion's insect weaves;
Though weeds are tangled on the stream,
It still reflects my morning's beam.

And therefore love I such as smile
On these neglected songs,
Nor deem that flattery's needless wile
My opening bosom wrongs;
For who would trample, at my side,
A few pale buds, my garden's pride?

It may be that my scanty ore
Long years have washed away,
And where were golden sands before,
Is nought but common clay;
Still something sparkles in the sun
For Memory to look back upon.

And when my name no more is heard,
    My lyre no more is known,
Still let me, like a winter's bird,
    In silence and alone,
Fold over them the weary wing
Once flashing through the dews of spring.

Yes, let my fancy fondly wrap
    My youth in its decline,
And riot in the rosy lap
    Of thoughts that once were mine,
And give the worm my little store
When the last reader reads no more!

OUR YANKEE GIRLS.

Let greener lands and bluer skies,
If such the wide earth shows,
With fairer cheeks and brighter eyes,
Match us the star and rose;
The winds that lift the Georgian's veil,
Or wave Circassia's curls,
Waft to their shores the sultan's sail,—
Who buys our Yankee girls?

The gay grisette, whose fingers touch
Love's thousand chords so well;
The dark Italian, loving much,
But more than *one* can tell;
And England's fair-haired, blue-eyed dame,
Who binds her brow with pearls;—
Ye who have seen them, can they shame
Our own sweet Yankee girls?

And what if court or castle vaunt
 Its children loftier born?—
Who heeds the silken tassel's flaunt
 Beside the golden corn?
They ask not for the dainty toil
 Of ribboned knights and earls,
The daughters of the virgin soil,
 Our freeborn Yankee girls!

By every hill whose stately pines
 Wave their dark arms above
The home where some fair being shines,
 To warm the wilds with love,
From barest rock to bleakest shore
 Where farthest sail unfurls,
That stars and stripes are streaming o'er,—
 God bless our Yankee girls!

LA GRISETTE.

Ah Clemence! when I saw thee last
    Trip down the Rue de Seine,
And turning, when thy form had past,
    I said, "We meet again," —
I dreamed not in that idle glance
    Thy latest image came,
And only left to memory's trance
    A shadow and a name.

The few strange words my lips had taught
    Thy timid voice to speak,
Their gentler signs, which often brought
    Fresh roses to thy cheek,
The trailing of thy long loose hair
    Bent o'er my couch of pain,
All, all returned, more sweet, more fair;
    O had we met again!

I walked where saint and virgin keep
    The vigil lights of Heaven,
I knew that thou hadst woes to weep,
    And sins to be forgiven;
I watched where Genevieve was laid,
    I knelt by Mary's shrine,
Beside me low, soft voices prayed;
    Alas! but where was thine?

And when the morning sun was bright,
    When wind and wave were calm,
And flamed, in thousand-tinted light,
    The rose of Notre Dame,
I wandered through the haunts of men,
    From Boulevard to Quai,
Till, frowning o'er Saint Etienne,
    The Pantheon's shadow lay.

In vain, in vain; we meet no more,
    Nor dream what fates befall;
And long upon the stranger's shore
    My voice on thee may call,
When years have clothed the line in moss,
    That tells thy name and days,
And withered, on thy simple cross,
    The wreaths of Père-la-Chaise!

AN EVENING THOUGHT.

WRITTEN AT SEA.

If sometimes in the dark blue eye,
Or in the deep red wine,
Or soothed by gentlest melody,
Still warms this heart of mine,
Yet something colder in the blood,
And calmer in the brain,
Have whispered that my youth's bright flood
Ebbs, not to flow again.

If by Helvetia's azure lake,
Or Arno's yellow stream,
Each star of memory could awake,
As in my first young dream,
I know that when mine eye shall greet
The hill-sides bleak and bare,
That gird my home, it will not meet
My childhood's sunsets there.

O when love's first, sweet, stolen kiss
Burned on my boyish brow,
Was that young forehead worn as this?
Was that flushed cheek as now?
Were that wild pulse and throbbing heart
Like these, which vainly strive,
In thankless strains of soulless art,
To dream themselves alive?

Alas! the morning dew is gone,
Gone ere the full of day;
Life's iron fetter still is on,
Its wreaths all torn away;
Happy if still some casual hour
Can warm the fading shrine,
Too soon to chill beyond the power
Of love, or song, or wine!

A SOUVENIR

Yes, lady! I can ne'er forget,
That once in other years we met;
Thy memory may perchance recall
A festal eve, a rose-wreathed hall,
Its tapers' blaze, its mirrors' glance,
Its melting song, its ringing dance; —
Why, in thy dream of virgin joy,
Shouldst thou recall a pallid boy?

Thine eye had other forms to seek,
Why rest upon his bashful cheek?
With other tones thy heart was stirred,
Why waste on him a gentle word?
We parted, lady, — all night long
Thine ear to thrill with dance and song, —
And I — to weep that I was born
A thing thou scarce wouldst deign to scorn.

And, lady! now that years have past,
My bark has reached the shore at last;
The gales that filled her ocean wing
Have chilled and shrunk thy hasty spring,
And eye to eye, and brow to brow,
I stand before thy presence now;—
Thy lip is smoothed, thy voice is sweet,
Thy warm hand offered when we meet.

Nay, lady! 't is not now for me
To droop the lid or bend the knee.
I seek thee,—oh, thou dost not shun;
I speak,—thou listenest like a nun;
I ask thy smile,—thy lip uncurls,
Too liberal of its flashing pearls;
Thy tears,—thy lashes sink again,—
My Hebe turns to Magdalen!

O changing youth! that evening hour
Look down on ours,—the bud—the flower;
Thine faded in its virgin soil,
And mine was nursed in tears and toil;
Thy leaves were withering, one by one,
While mine were opening to the sun;—
Which now can meet the cold and storm,
With freshest leaf and hardiest form?

Ay, lady! that once haughty glance
Still wanders through the glittering dance,
And asks in vain from others' pride,
The charity thine own denied;
And as thy fickle lips could learn
To smile and praise,—that used to spurn,
So the last offering on thy shrine
Shall be this flattering lay of mine!

"QUI VIVE!"

"Qui vive!" The sentry's musket rings,
    The channelled bayonet gleams;
High o'er him, like a raven's wings
The broad tri-colored banner flings
Its shadow, rustling as it swings
    Pale in the moonlight beams;
Pass on! while steel-clad sentries keep
Their vigil o'er the monarch's sleep,
    Thy bare, unguarded breast
Asks not the unbroken, bristling zone
That girds yon sceptred trembler's throne;—
    Pass on, and take thy rest!

"*Qui vive!*" How oft the midnight air
    That startling cry has borne!
How oft the evening breeze has fanned
The banner of this haughty land,

O'er mountain snow and desert sand,
    Ere yet its folds were torn!
Through Jena's carnage flying red,
Or tossing o'er Marengo's dead,
    Or curling on the towers
Where Austria's eagle quivers yet,
And suns the ruffled plumage, wet
    With battle's crimson showers!

"*Qui vive!*" And is the sentry's cry, —
    The sleepless soldier's hand, —
Are these, — the painted folds that fly
And lift their emblems, printed high,
On morning mist and sunset sky, —
    The guardians of a land?
No! If the patriot's pulses sleep,
How vain the watch that hirelings keep, —
    The idle flag that waves,
When Conquest, with his iron heel,
Treads down the standards and the steel
    That belt the soil of slaves!

THE WASP AND THE HORNET.

THE two proud sisters of the sea,
In glory and in doom! —
Well may the eternal waters be
Their broad, unsculptured tomb!
The wind that rings along the wave,
The clear, unshadowed sun,
Are torch and trumpet o'er the brave,
Whose last green wreath is won!

No stranger-hand their banners furled,
No victor's shout they heard;
Unseen, above them ocean curled,
Save by his own pale bird;
The gnashing billows heaved and fell;
Wild shrieked the midnight gale;
Far, far beneath the morning swell
Were pennon, spar, and sail.

The land of Freedom! Sea and shore
    Are guarded now, as when
Her ebbing waves to victory bore
    Fair barks and gallant men;
O many a ship of prouder name
    May wave her starry fold,
Nor trail, with deeper light of fame,
    The paths they swept of old!

FROM A BACHELOR'S PRIVATE JOURNAL.

Sweet Mary, I have never breathed
The love it were in vain to name;
Though round my heart a serpent wreathed,
I smiled, or strove to smile, the same.

Once more the pulse of Nature glows
With faster throb and fresher fire,
While music round her pathway flows
Like echoes from a hidden lyre.

And is there none with me to share
The glories of the earth and sky?
The eagle through the pathless air
Is followed by one burning eye.

Ah no! the cradled flowers may wake,
Again may flow the frozen sea,
From every cloud a star may break,—
There comes no second Spring to me.

Go, — ere the painted toys of youth
Are crushed beneath the tread of years;
Ere visions have been chilled to truth,
And hopes are washed away in tears.

Go, — for I will not bid thee weep, —
Too soon my sorrows will be thine,
And evening's troubled air shall sweep
The incense from the broken shrine.

If Heaven can hear the dying tone
Of chords that soon will cease to thrill,
The prayer that Heaven has heard alone,
May bless thee when those chords are still.

STANZAS.

STRANGE! that one lightly-whispered tone
Is far, far sweeter unto me.
Than all the sounds that kiss the earth,
Or breathe along the sea;
But, lady, when thy voice I greet,
Not heavenly music seems so sweet.

I look upon the fair blue skies,
And nought but empty air I see;
But when I turn me to thine eyes,
It seemeth unto me
Ten thousand angels spread their wings
Within those little azure rings.

The lily hath the softest leaf
That ever western breeze hath fanned,
But thou shalt have the tender flower,
So I may take thy hand;
That little hand to me doth yield
More joy than all the broidered field.

O lady! there be many things
    That seem right fair, below, above;
But sure not one among them all
    Is half so sweet as love;—
Let us not pay our vows alone,
But join two altars both in one.

THE PHILOSOPHER TO HIS LOVE.

Dearest, a look is but a ray
Reflected in a certain way;
A word, whatever tone it wear,
Is but a trembling wave of air;
A touch, obedience to a clause
In nature's pure material laws.

The very flowers that bend and meet,
In sweetening others, grow more sweet;
The clouds by day, the stars by night,
Inweave their floating locks of light;
The rainbow, Heaven's own forehead's braid,
Is but the embrace of sun and shade.

How few that love us have we found!
How wide the world that girds them round'
Like mountain streams we meet.and part,
Each living in the other's heart,
Our course unknown, our hope to be
Yet mingled in the distant sea.

But Ocean coils and heaves in vain,
Bound in the subtle moonbeam's chain;
And love and hope do but obey
Some cold, capricious planet's ray,
Which lights and leads the tide it charms,
To Death's dark caves and icy arms.

Alas! one narrow line is drawn,
That links our sunset with our dawn;
In mist and shade life's morning rose,
And clouds are round it at its close;
But ah! no twilight beam ascends
To whisper where that evening ends.

Oh! in the hour when I shall feel
Those shadows round my senses steal,
When gentle eyes are weeping o'er
The clay that feels their tears no more,
Then let thy spirit with me be,
Or some sweet angel, likest thee!

L'INCONNUE.

Is thy name Mary, maiden fair?
    Such should, methinks, its music be;
The sweetest name that mortals bear,
    Were best befitting thee;
And she, to whom it once was given,
Was half of earth and half of heaven

I hear thy voice, I see thy smile,
    I look upon thy folded hair;
Ah! while we dream not they beguile,
    Our hearts are in the snare;
And she, who chains a wild bird's wing,
Must start not if her captive sing.

So, lady, take the leaf that falls,
    To all but thee unseen, unknown;
When evening shades thy silent walls,
    Then read it all alone;
In stillness read, in darkness seal,
Forget, despise, but not reveal!

THE STAR AND THE WATER-LILY.

THE sun stepped down from his golden throne,
    And lay in the silent sea,
And the Lily had folded her satin leaves,
    For a sleepy thing was she;
What is the Lily dreaming of?
    Why crisp the waters blue?
See, see, she is lifting her varnished lid!
    Her white leaves are glistening through!

The Rose is cooling his burning cheek
    In the lap of the breathless tide;—
The Lily hath sisters fresh and fair,
    That would lie by the Rose's side;
He would love her better than all the rest,
    And he would be fond and true;—
But the Lily unfolded her weary lids,
    And looked at the sky so blue.

Remember, remember, thou silly one,
How fast will thy summer glide,
And wilt thou wither a virgin pale,
Or flourish a blooming bride?
"O the Rose is old, and thorny, and cold,
And he lives on earth," said she;
"But the Star is fair and he lives in the air,
And he shall my bridegroom be."

But what if the stormy cloud should come,
And ruffle the silver sea?
Would he turn his eye from the distant sky,
To smile on a thing like thee?
O no, fair Lily, he will not send
One ray from his far-off throne;
The winds shall blow and the waves shall flow,
And thou wilt be left alone.

There is not a leaf on the mountain top,
Nor a drop of evening dew,
Nor a golden sand on the sparkling shore,
Nor a pearl in the waters blue,
That he has not cheered with his fickle smile,
And warmed with his faithless beam.—
And will he be true to a pallid flower,
That floats on the quiet stream?

Alas for the Lily! she would not heed,
    But turned to the skies afar,
And bared her breast to the trembling ray
    That shot from the rising star;
The cloud came over the darkened sky,
    And over the waters wide:
She looked in vain through the beating rain,
    And sank in the stormy tide.

ILLUSTRATION OF A PICTURE.

"A SPANISH GIRL IN REVERIE."

She twirled the string of golden beads,
That round her neck was hung, —
My grandsire's gift; the good old man
Loved girls when he was young;
And, bending lightly o'er the cord,
And turning half away,
With something like a youthful sigh,
Thus spoke the maiden gray:

"Well, one may trail her silken robe,
And bind her locks with pearls,
And one may wreathe the woodland rose
Among her floating curls;
And one may tread the dewy grass,
And one the marble floor,
Nor half-hid bosom heave the less,
Nor broidered corset more!

"Some years ago, a dark-eyed girl
Was sitting in the shade, —
There 's something brings her to my mind
In that young dreaming maid, —
And in her hand she held a flower,
A flower, whose speaking hue
Said, in the language of the heart,
'Believe the giver true.'

"And, as she looked upon its leaves,
The maiden made a vow
To wear it when the bridal wreath
Was woven for her brow;
She watched the flower, as, day by day,
The leaflets curled and died;
But he who gave it never came
To claim her for his bride.

"O many a summer's morning glow
Has lent the rose its ray,
And many a winter's drifting snow
Has swept its bloom away;
But she has kept that faithless pledge
To this, her winter hour,
And keeps it still, herself alone,
And wasted like the flower."

Her pale lip quivered, and the light
Gleamed in her moistening eyes ; —
I asked her how she liked the tints
In those Castilian skies ?
" She thought them misty, — 't was perhaps
Because she stood too near ; "
She turned away, and as she turned,
I saw her wipe a tear.

THE DYING SENECA.

HE died not as the martyr dies,
Wrapped in his living shroud of flame;
He fell not as the warrior falls,
Gasping upon the field of fame;
A gentler passage to the grave,
The murderer's softened fury gave.

Rome's slaughtered sons and blazing piles
Had tracked the purple demon's path,
And yet another victim lived
To fill the fiery scroll of wrath;
Could not imperial vengeance spare
His furrowed brow and silver hair?

The field was sown with noble blood,
The harvest reaped in burning tears,
When, rolling up its crimson flood,
Broke the long-gathering tide of years;
His diadem was rent away,
And beggars trampled on his clay.

None wept, — none pitied ; — they who knelt
    At morning by the despot's throne,
At evening dashed the laurelled bust,
    And spurned the wreaths themselves had strewn ;
The shout of triumph echoed wide,
The self-stung reptile writhed and died !

A PORTRAIT.

A STILL, sweet, placid, moonlight face,
    And slightly nonchalant,
Which seems to claim a middle place
    Between one's love and aunt,
Where childhood's star has left a ray
    In woman's sunniest sky,
As morning dew and blushing day
    On fruit and blossom lie.

And yet, — and yet I cannot love
    Those lovely lines on steel;
They beam too much of heaven above,
    Earth's darker shades to feel;
Perchance some early weeds of care
    Around my heart have grown,
And brows unfurrowed seem not fair,
    Because they mock my own.

Alas! when Eden's gates were sealed,
    How oft some sheltered flower
Breathed o'er the wanderers of the field,
    Like their own bridal bower;
Yet, saddened by its loveliness,
    And humbled by its pride,
Earth's fairest child they could not bless, —
    It mocked them when they sighed.

A ROMAN AQUEDUCT.

THE sun-browned girl, whose limbs recline
    When noon her languid hand has laid
Hot on the green flakes of the pine,
    Beneath its narrow disk of shade;

As, through the flickering noontide glare,
    She gazes on the rainbow chain
Of arches, lifting once in air
    The rivers of the Roman's plain; —

Say, does her wandering eye recall
    The mountain-current's icy wave, —
Or for the dead one tear let fall,
    Whose founts are broken by their grave?

From stone to stone the ivy weaves
    Her braided tracery's winding veil,
And lacing stalks and tangled leaves
    Nod heavy in the drowsy gale.

And lightly floats the pendent vine,
    That swings beneath her slender bow,
Arch answering arch, — whose rounded line
    Seems mirrored in the wreath below.

How patient Nature smiles at Fame!
    The weeds, that strewed the victor's way,
Feed on his dust to shroud his name,
    Green where his proudest towers decay.

See, through that channel, empty now,
    The scanty rain its tribute pours, —
Which cooled the lip and laved the brow
    Of conquerors from a hundred shores.

Thus bending o'er the nation's bier,
    Whose wants the captive earth supplied,
The dew of Memory's passing tear
    Falls on the arches of her pride!

THE LAST PROPHECY OF CASSANDRA.

THE sun is fading in the skies
    And evening shades are gathering fast;
Fair city, ere that sun shall rise,
    Thy night hath come, — thy day is past!

Ye know not, — but the hour is nigh;
    Ye will not heed the warning breath;
No vision strikes your clouded eye,
    To break the sleep that wakes in death.

Go, age, and let thy withered cheek
    Be wet once more with freezing tears;
And bid thy trembling sorrow speak,
    In accents of departed years.

Go, child, and pour thy sinless prayer
    Before the everlasting throne;
And He who sits in glory there,
    May stoop to hear thy silver tone.

Go, warrior, in thy glittering steel,
And bow thee at the altar's side;
And bid thy frowning gods reveal
The doom their mystic counsels hide.

Go, maiden, in thy flowing veil,
And bare thy brow, and bend thy knee;
When the last hopes of mercy fail,
Thy God may yet remember thee.

Go, as thou didst in happier hours,
And lay thine incense on the shrine;
And greener leaves, and fairer flowers,
Around the sacred image twine.

I saw them rise, — the buried dead, —
From marble tomb and grassy mound;
I heard the spirits' printless tread,
And voices not of earthly sound.

I looked upon the quivering stream,
And its cold wave was bright with flame;
And wild, as from a fearful dream,
The wasted forms of battle came.

Ye will not hear, — ye will not know, —
    Ye scorn the maniac's idle song;
Ye care not! but the voice of woe
    Shall thunder loud, and echo long.

Blood shall be in your marble halls,
    And spears shall glance, and fires shall glow;
Ruin shall sit upon your walls,
    But ye shall lie in death below.

Ay, none shall live to hear the storm
    Around their blackened pillars sweep;
To shudder at the reptile's form,
    Or scare the wild bird from her sleep.

TO A CAGED LION.

Poor conquered monarch! though that haughty glance
 Still speaks thy courage unsubdued by time,
And in the grandeur of thy sullen tread
 Lives the proud spirit of thy burning clime; —
Fettered by things that shudder at thy roar,
Torn from thy pathless wilds to pace this narrow floor!

Thou wast the victor, and all nature shrunk
 Before the thunders of thine awful wrath;
The steel-armed hunter viewed thee from afar,
 Fearless and trackless in thy lonely path!
The famished tiger closed his flaming eye,
And crouched and panted as thy step went by!

Thou art the vanquished, and insulting man
 Bars thy broad bosom as a sparrow's wing;
His nerveless arms thine iron sinews bind,
 And lead in chains the desert's fallen king;
Are these the beings that have dared to twine
Their feeble threads around those limbs of thine?

So must it be; the weaker, wiser race,
    That wields the tempest and that rides the sea,
Even in the stillness of thy solitude
    Must teach the lesson of its power to thee;
And thou, the terror of the trembling wild,
Must bow thy savage strength, the mockery of a child!

TO MY COMPANIONS.

Mine ancient Chair! thy wide-embracing arms
Have clasped around me even from a boy;
Hadst thou a voice to speak of years gone by,
Thine were a tale of sorrow and of joy,
Of fevered hopes and ill-foreboding fears,
And smiles unseen, and unrecorded tears.

And thou, my Table! though unwearied Time
Hath set his signet on thine altered brow,
Still can I see thee in thy spotless prime,
And in my memory thou art living now;
Soon must thou slumber with forgotten things,
The peasant's ashes and the dust of kings.

Thou melancholy Mug! thy sober brown
Hath something pensive in its evening hue,
Not like the things that please the tasteless clown,
With gaudy streaks of orange and of blue;
And I must love thee, for thou art mine own,
Pressed by my lip, and pressed by mine alone.

My broken Mirror! faithless, yet beloved,
    Thou who canst smile, and smile alike on all,
Oft do I leave thee, oft again return,
    I scorn the siren, but obey the call;
I hate thy falsehood, while I fear thy truth,
But most I love thee, flattering friend of youth.

Primeval Carpet! every well-worn thread
    Has slowly parted with its virgin dye;
I saw thee fade beneath the ceaseless tread,
    Fainter and fainter in mine anxious eye
So flies the color from the brightest flower,
And heaven's own rainbow lives but for an hour.

I love you all! there radiates from our own
    A soul that lives in every shape we see;
There is a voice, to other ears unknown,
    Like echoed music answering to its key.
The dungeoned captive hath a tale to tell,
Of every insect in his lonely cell;
And these poor frailties have a simple tone,
That breathes in accents sweet to me alone.

THE LAST LEAF.

I SAW him once before,
As he passed by the door,
    And again
The pavement stones resound,
As he totters o'er the ground
    With his cane.

They say that in his prime,
Ere the pruning-knife of Time
    Cut him down,
Not a better man was found
By the Crier on his round
    Through the town.

But now he walks the streets,
And he looks at all he meets
    Sad and wan,
And he shakes his feeble head,
That it seems as if he said,
    "They are gone."

The mossy marbles rest
On the lips that he has prest
    In their bloom,
And the names he loved to hear
Have been carved for many a year
    On the tomb.

My grandmamma has said,—
Poor old lady, she is dead
    Long ago,—
That he had a Roman nose,
And his cheek was like a rose
    In the snow.

But now his nose is thin,
And it rests upon his chin
    Like a staff,
And a crook is in his back,
And a melancholy crack
    In his laugh.

I know it is a sin
For me to sit and grin
    At him here;
But the old three-cornered hat,
And the breeches, and all that,
    Are so queer!

And if I should live to be
The last leaf upon the tree
  In the spring, —
Let them smile, as I do now,
At the old forsaken bough
  Where I cling.

TO A BLANK SHEET OF PAPER.

Wan-visaged thing! thy virgin leaf
To me looks more than deadly pale,
Unknowing what may stain thee yet, —
A poem or a tale.

Who can thy unborn meaning scan?
Can Seer or Sibyl read thee now?
No, — seek to trace the fate of man
Writ on his infant brow.

Love may light on thy snowy cheek,
And shake his Eden-breathing plumes
Then shalt thou tell how Lelia smiles,
Or Angelina blooms.

Satire may lift his bearded lance,
Forestalling Time's slow-moving scythe,
And, scattered on thy little field,
Disjointed bards may writhe.

Perchance a vision of the night,
Some grizzled spectre, gaunt and thin,
Or sheeted corpse, may stalk along,
Or skeleton may grin!

If it should be in pensive hour
Some sorrow-moving theme I try,
Ah, maiden, how thy tears will fall,
For all I doom to die!

But if in merry mood I touch
Thy leaves, then shall the sight of thee
Sow smiles as thick on rosy lips
As ripples on the sea.

The Weekly press shall gladly stoop
To bind thee up among its sheaves;
The Daily steal thy shining ore,
To gild its leaden leaves.

Thou hast no tongue, yet thou canst speak,
Till distant shores shall hear the sound;
Thou hast no life, yet thou canst breathe
Fresh life on all around.

Thou art the arena of the wise,
The noiseless battle-ground of fame;
The sky where halos may be wreathed
Around the humblest name.

Take, then, this treasure to thy trust,
To win some idle reader's smile,
Then fade and moulder in the dust,
Or swell some bonfire's crackling pile!

TO AN INSECT.

I love to hear thine earnest voice,
　　Wherever thou art hid,
Thou testy little dogmatist,
　　Thou pretty Katydid!
Thou mindest me of gentlefolks,—
　　Old gentlefolks are they,—
Thou say'st an undisputed thing
　　In such a solemn way.

Thou art a female, Katydid!
　　I know it by the trill
That quivers through thy piercing notes,
　　So petulant and shrill.
I think there is a knot of you
　　Beneath the hollow tree,—
A knot of spinster Katydids,—
　　Do Katydids drink tea?

O tell me where did Katy live,
And what did Katy do?
And was she very fair and young,
And yet so wicked, too?
Did Katy love a naughty man,
Or kiss more cheeks than one?
I warrant Katy did no more
Than many a Kate has done.

Dear me! I 'll tell you all about
My fuss with little Jane,
And Ann, with whom I used to walk
So often down the lane,
And all that tore their locks of black,
Or wet their eyes of blue,—
Pray tell me, sweetest Katydid,
What did poor Katy do?

Ah no! the living oak shall crash,
That stood for ages still,
The rock shall rend its mossy base
And thunder down the hill,
Before the little Katydid
Shall add one word, to tell
The mystic story of the maid
Whose name she knows so well.

Peace to the ever-murmuring race!
    And when the latest one
Shall fold in death her feeble wings
    Beneath the autumn sun,
Then shall she raise her fainting voice
    And lift her drooping lid,
And then the child of future years
    Shall hear what Katy did.

THE DILEMMA.

Now, by the blessed Paphian queen,
Who heaves the breast of sweet sixteen;
By every name I cut on bark
Before my morning star grew dark;
By Hymen's torch, by Cupid's dart,
By all that thrills the beating heart;
The bright black eye, the melting blue,—
I cannot choose between the two.

I had a vision in my dreams;—
I saw a row of twenty beams;
From every beam a rope was hung,
In every rope a lover swung;
I asked the hue of every eye,
That bade each luckless lover die;
Ten shadowy lips said, heavenly blue,
And ten accused the darker hue.

I asked a matron, which she deemed
With fairest light of beauty beamed;
She answered, some thought both were fair,—
Give her blue eyes and golden hair.
I might have liked her judgment well,
But, as she spoke, she rung the bell,
And all her girls, nor small nor few,
Came marching in,—their eyes were blue.

I asked a maiden; back she flung
The locks that round her forehead hung,
And turned her eye, a glorious one,
Bright as a diamond in the sun,
On me, until beneath its rays
I felt as if my hair would blaze;
She liked all eyes but eyes of green;
She looked at me; what could she mean?

Ah! many lids Love lurks between,
Nor heeds the coloring of his screen;
And when his random arrows fly,
The victim falls, but knows not why.
Gaze not upon his shield of jet,
The shaft upon the string is set;
Look not beneath his azure veil,
Though every limb were cased in mail.

Well, both might make a martyr break
The chain that bound him to the stake;
And both, with but a single ray,
Can melt our very hearts away;
And both, when balanced, hardly seem
To stir the scales, or rock the beam;
But that is dearest, all the while,
That wears for us the sweetest smile.

MY AUNT

My aunt! my dear unmarried aunt!
Long years have o'er her flown;
Yet still she strains the aching clasp
That binds her virgin zone;
I know it hurts her, — though she looks
As cheerful as she can;
Her waist is ampler than her life,
For life is but a span.

My aunt! my poor deluded aunt!
Her hair is almost gray;
Why will she train that winter curl
In such a spring-like way?
How can she lay her glasses down,
And say she reads as well,
When, through a double convex lens,
She just makes out to spell?

Her father, — grandpapa! forgive
This erring lip its smiles, —
Vowed she should make the finest gir.
Within a hundred miles;
He sent her to a stylish school;
'T was in her thirteenth June;
And with her, as the rules required,
"Two towels and a spoon."

They braced my aunt against a board,
To make her straight and tall;
They laced her up, they starved her down,
To make her light and small·
They pinched her feet, they singed her hair
They screwed it up with pins; —
O never mortal suffered more
In penance for her sins.

So, when my precious aunt was done,
My grandsire brought her back;
(By daylight, lest some rabid youth
Might follow on the track;)
"Ah!" said my grandsire, as he shook
Some powder in his pan,
"What could this lovely creature do
Against a desperate man!"

Alas! nor chariot, nor barouche,
    Nor bandit cavalcade,
Tore from the trembling father's arms
    His all-accomplished maid.
For her how happy had it been!
    And Heaven had spared to me
To see one sad, ungathered rose
    On my ancestral tree.

THE TOADSTOOL.

THERE 's a thing that grows by the fainting flower,
And springs in the shade of the lady's bower;
The lily shrinks, and the rose turns pale,
When they feel its breath in the summer gale,
And the tulip curls its leaves in pride,
And the blue-eyed violet starts aside;
But the lily may flaunt, and the tulip stare,
For what does the honest toadstool care?

She does not glow in a painted vest,
And she never blooms on the maiden's breast;
But she comes, as the saintly sisters do,
In a modest suit of a Quaker hue.
And, when the stars in the evening skies
Are weeping dew from their gentle eyes,
The toad comes out from his hermit cell,
The tale of his faithful love to tell.

O there is light in her lover's glance,
That flies to her heart like a silver lance;
His breeches are made of spotted skin,
His jacket is tight, and his pumps are thin;
In a cloudless night you may hear his song,
As its pensive melody floats along,
And, if you will look by the moonlight fair,
The trembling form of the toad is there.

And he twines his arms round her slender stem,
In the shade of her velvet diadem;
But she turns away in her maiden shame,
And will not breathe on the kindling flame;
He sings at her feet through the livelong night,
And creeps to his cave at the break of light;
And whenever he comes to the air above,
His throat is swelling with baffled love.

THE MEETING OF THE DRYADS.*

It was not many centuries since,
    When, gathered on the moonlit green,
Beneath the Tree of Liberty,
    A ring of weeping sprites was seen.

The freshman's lamp had long been dim,
    The voice of busy day was mute,
And tortured melody had ceased
    Her sufferings on the evening flute.

They met not as they once had met,
    To laugh o'er many a jocund tale;
But every pulse was beating low,
    And every cheek was cold and pale.

There rose a fair but faded one,
    Who oft had cheered them with her song;
She waved a mutilated arm,
    And silence held the listening throng.

---

* Written after a general pruning of the trees around Harvard College.

"Sweet friends," the gentle nymph began,
"From opening bud to withering leaf,
One common lot has bound us all,
In every change of joy and grief.

"While all around has felt decay,
We rose in ever-living prime,
With broader shade and fresher green,
Beneath the crumbling step of Time.

"When often by our feet has past
Some biped, nature's walking whim,
Say, have we trimmed one awkward shape,
Or lopped away one crooked limb?

"Go on, fair Science; soon to thee
Shall Nature yield her idle boast;
Her vulgar fingers formed a tree,
But thou hast trained it to a post.

"Go paint the birch's silver rind,
And quilt the peach with softer down;
Up with the willow's trailing threads,
Off with the sunflower's radiant crown!

"Go, plant the lily on the shore,
And set the rose among the waves,
And bid the tropic bud unbind
Its silken zone in arctic caves;

"Bring bellows for the panting winds,
Hang up a lantern by the moon,
And give the nightingale a fife,
And lend the eagle a balloon!

"I cannot smile,—the tide of scorn,
That rolled through every bleeding vein,
Comes kindling fiercer as it flows
Back to its burning source again.

"Again in every quivering leaf
That moment's agony I feel,
When limbs, that spurned the northern blast,
Shrunk from the sacrilegious steel.

"A curse upon the wretch who dared
To crop us with his felon saw!
May every fruit his lip shall taste
Lie like a bullet in his maw.

"In every julep that he drinks,
  May gout, and bile, and headache be;
And when he strives to calm his pain,
  May colic mingle with his tea.

"May nightshade cluster round his path,
  And thistles shoot, and brambles cling;
May blistering ivy scorch his veins,
  And dogwood burn, and nettles sting.

"On him may never shadow fall,
  When fever racks his throbbing brow,
And his last shilling buy a rope
  To hang him on my highest bough!"

She spoke;—the morning's herald beam
  Sprang from the bosom of the sea,
And every mangled sprite returned
  In sadness to her wounded tree.*

---

* A little poem, on a similar occasion, may be found in the works of Swift, from which, perhaps, the idea was borrowed; although I was as much surprised as amused to meet with it some time after writing the preceding lines.

THE MYSTERIOUS VISITER.

There was a sound of hurrying feet,
A tramp on echoing stairs,
There was a rush along the aisles, —
It was the hour of prayers.

And on, like Ocean's midnight wave,
The current rolled along,
When, suddenly, a stranger form
Was seen amidst the throng.

He was a dark and swarthy man
That uninvited guest;
A faded coat of bottle green
Was buttoned round his breast.

There was not one among them all
Could say from whence he came;
Nor beardless boy, nor ancient man,
Could tell that stranger's name.

All silent as the sheeted dead,
    In spite of sneer and frown,
Fast by a gray-haired senior's side
    He sat him boldly down.

There was a look of horror flashed
    From out the tutor's eyes;
When all around him rose to pray,
    The stranger did not rise!

A murmur broke along the crowd,
    The prayer was at an end;
With ringing heels and measured tread
    A hundred forms descend.

Through sounding aisle, o'er grating stair,
    The long procession poured,
Till all were gathered on the seats
    Around the Commons board.

That fearful stranger! down he sat,
    Unasked, yet undismayed;
And on his lip a rising smile
    Of scorn or pleasure played.

He took his hat and hung it up,
With slow but earnest air;
He stripped his coat from off his back,
And placed it on a chair.

Then from his nearest neighbor's side
A knife and plate he drew;
And, reaching out his hand again,
He took his teacup too.

How fled the sugar from the bowl!
How sunk the azure cream!
They vanished like the shapes that float
Upon a summer's dream.

A long, long draught, — an outstretched hand, —
And crackers, toast, and tea,
They faded from the stranger's touch
Like dew upon the sea.

Then clouds were dark on many a brow,
Fear sat upon their souls,
And, in a bitter agony,
They clasped their buttered rolls.

A whisper trembled through the crowd,—
Who could the stranger be?
And some were silent, for they thougnt
A cannibal was he.

What if the creature should arise,—
For he was stout and tall,—
And swallow down a sophomore,
Coat, crow's-foot, cap, and all!

All sullenly the stranger rose;
They sat in mute despair;
He took his hat from off the peg,
His coat from off the chair.

Four freshmen fainted on the seat,
Six swooned upon the floor;
Yet on the fearful being passed,
And shut the chapel door.

There is full many a starving man,
That walks in bottle green,
But never more that hungry one
In Commons-hall was seen.

Yet often at the sunset hour,
    When tolls the evening bell,
The freshman lingers on the steps,
    That frightful tale to tell.

THE SPECTRE PIG.

A BALLAD.

It was the stalwart butcher man,
    That knit his swarthy brow,
And said the gentle Pig must die,
    And sealed it with a vow.

And oh! it was the gentle Pig
    Lay stretched upon the ground,
And ah! it was the cruel knife
    His little heart that found.

They took him then, those wicked men,
    They trailed him all along;
They put a stick between his lips,
    And through his heels a thong;

And round and round an oaken beam
 A hempen cord they flung,
And, like a mighty pendulum,
 All solemnly he swung!

Now say thy prayers, thou sinful man,
 And think what thou hast done,
And read thy catechism well,
 Thou bloody-minded one;

For if his sprite should walk by night,
 It better were for thee,
That thou wert mouldering in the ground,
 Or bleaching in the sea.

It was the savage butcher then,
 That made a mock of sin,
And swore a very wicked oath,
 He did not care a pin.

It was the butcher's youngest son, —
 His voice was broke with sighs,
And with his pocket handkerchief
 He wiped his little eyes;

All young and ignorant was he,
    But innocent and mild,
And, in his soft simplicity,
    Out spoke the tender child ; —

" O father, father, list to me ;
    The Pig is deadly sick,
And men have hung him by his heels,
    And fed him with a stick."

It was the bloody butcher then,
    That laughed as he would die,
Yet did he soothe the sorrowing child,
    And bid him not to cry ; —

" O Nathan, Nathan, what 's a Pig,
    That thou shouldst weep and wail ?
Come, bear thee like a butcher's child,
    And thou shalt have his tail ! "

It was the butcher's daughter then,
    So slender and so fair,
That sobbed as if her heart would break,
    And tore her yellow hair ;

And thus she spoke in thrilling tone,—
    Fast fell the tear-drops big;—
"Ah! woe is me! Alas! Alas!
    The Pig! The Pig! The Pig!"

Then did her wicked father's lips
    Make merry with her woe,
And call her many a naughty name,
    Because she whimpered so.

Ye need not weep, ye gentle ones,
    In vain your tears are shed,
Ye cannot wash his crimson hand,
    Ye cannot soothe the dead.

The bright sun folded on his breast
    His robes of rosy flame,
And softly over all the west
    The shades of evening came.

He slept, and troops of murdered Pigs
    Were busy with his dreams;
Loud rang their wild, unearthly shrieks,
    Wide yawned their mortal seams.

The clock struck twelve; the Dead hath heard;
He opened both his eyes,
And sullenly he shook his tail
To lash the feeding flies.

One quiver of the hempen cord, —
One struggle and one bound, —
With stiffened limb and leaden eye,
The Pig was on the ground!

And straight towards the sleeper's house
His fearful way he wended;
And hooting owl, and hovering bat,
On midnight wing attended

Back flew the bolt, up rose the latch,
And open swung the door,
And little mincing feet were heard
Pat, pat along the floor.

Two hoofs upon the sanded floor,
And two upon the bed;
And they are breathing side by side,
The living and the dead!

"Now wake, now wake, thou butcher man!
What makes thy cheek so pale?
Take hold! take hold! thou dost not fear
To clasp a spectre's tail?"

Untwisted every winding coil;
The shuddering wretch took hold,
All like an icicle it seemed,
So tapering and so cold.

"Thou com'st with me, thou butcher man!" —
He strives to loose his grasp,
But, faster than the clinging vine,
Those twining spirals clasp.

And open, open swung the door,
And, fleeter than the wind,
The shadowy spectre swept before,
The butcher trailed behind.

Fast fled the darkness of the night,
And morn rose faint and dim;
They called full loud, they knocked full long,
They did not waken him.

Straight, straight towards that oaken beam,
    A trampled pathway ran;
A ghastly shape was swinging there,—
    It was the butcher man.

LINES BY A CLERK.

Oh! I did love her dearly,
    And gave her toys and rings,
And I thought she meant sincerely,
    When she took my pretty things
But her heart has grown as icy
    As a fountain in the fall,
And her love, that was so spicy,
    It did not last at all.

I gave her once a locket,
    It was filled with my own hair,
And she put it in her pocket
    With very special care.
But a jeweller has got it, —
    He offered it to me,
And another that is not it
    Around her neck I see.

For my cooings and my billings
I do not now complain,
But my dollars and my shillings
Will never come again;
They were earned with toil and sorrow,
But I never told her that,
And now I have to borrow,
And want another hat.

Think, think, thou cruel Emma,
When thou shalt hear my woe,
And know my sad dilemma,
That thou hast made it so.
See, see my beaver rusty,
Look, look upon this hole,
This coat is dim and dusty;
O let it rend thy soul!

Before the gates of fashion
I daily bent my knee,
But I sought the shrine of passion,
And found my idol, — thee;
Though never love intenser
Had bowed a soul before it,
Thine eye was on the censer,
And not the hand that bore it.

REFLECTIONS OF A PROUD PEDESTRIAN.

I SAW the curl of his waving lash,
 And the glance of his knowing eye,
And I knew that he thought he was cutting a dash,
 As his steed went thundering by.

And he may ride in the rattling gig,
 Or flourish the Stanhope gay,
And dream that he looks exceeding big
 To the people that walk in the way;

But he shall think, when the night is still,
 On the stable-boy's gathering numbers,
And the ghost of many a veteran bill
 Shall hover around his slumbers;

The ghastly dun shall worry his sleep,
 And constables cluster around him,
And he shall creep from the wood-hole deep
 Where their spectre eyes have found him!

Ay! gather your reins, and crack your thong,
And bid your steed go faster;
He does not know, as he scrambles along,
That he has a fool for his master;

And hurry away on your lonely ride,
Nor deign from the mire to save me;
I will paddle it stoutly at your side
With the tandem that nature gave me!

THE POET'S LOT.

WHAT is a poet's love ?—
    To write a girl a sonnet
To get a ring, or some such thing,
    And fustianize upon it.

What is a poet's fame ?—
    Sad hints about his reason,
And sadder praise from garreteers,
    To be returned in season.

Where go the poet's lines ?—
    Answer, ye evening tapers !
Ye auburn locks, ye golden curls,
    Speak from your folded papers !

Child of the ploughshare, smile ;
    Boy of the counter, grieve not,
Though muses round thy trundle-bed
    Their broidered tissue weave not.

The poet's future holds
    No civic wreath above him ;
Nor slated roof, nor varnished chaise,
    Nor wife nor child to love him.

Maid of the village inn,
    Who workest woe on satin,
(The grass in black, the graves in green,
    The epitaph in Latin,)

Trust not to them who say
    In stanzas, they adore thee ;
O rather sleep in church-yard clay,
    With urns and cherubs o'er thee !

DAILY TRIALS.

BY A SENSITIVE MAN.

O THERE are times
When all this fret and tumult that we hear
Do seem more stale than to the sexton's ear
His own dull chimes.

Ding dong! ding dong!
The world is in a simmer like a sea
Over a pent volcano, — woe is me
All the day long!

From crib to shroud!
Nurse o'er our cradles screameth lullaby,
And friends in boots tramp round us as we die.
Snuffling aloud.

At morning's call
The small-voiced pug-dog welcomes in the sun,
And flea-bit mongrels, wakening one by one,
Give answer all.

When evening dim
Draws round us, then the lonely caterwaul
Tart solo, sour duet, and general squall, —
These are our hymn.

Women, with tongues
Like polar needles, ever on the jar, —
Men, plugless word-spouts, whose deep fountains are
Within their lungs.

Children, with drums
Strapped round them by the fond paternal ass,
Peripatetics with a blade of grass
Between their thumbs.

Vagrants, whose arts
Have caged some devil in their mad machine,
Which grinding, squeaks, with husky groans between,
Come out by starts.

Cockneys that kill
Thin horses of a Sunday, — men, with clams,
Hoarse as young bisons roaring for their dams
From hill to hill.

Soldiers, with guns
Making a nuisance of the blessed air,
Child-crying bellmen, children in despair
Screeching for buns.

Storms, thunders, waves!
Howl, crash, and bellow till ye get your fill;
Ye sometimes rest; men never can be still
But in their graves.

EVENING.

BY A TAILOR.

Day hath put on his jacket, and around
His burning bosom buttoned it with stars.
Here will I lay me on the velvet grass,
That is like padding to earth's meagre ribs,
And hold communion with the things about me.
Ah me! how lovely is the golden braid,
That binds the skirt of night's descending robe!
The thin leaves, quivering on their silken threads,
Do make a music like to rustling satin,
As the light breezes smooth their downy nap.

Ha! what is this that rises to my touch,
So like a cushion? Can it be a cabbage?
It is, it is that deeply injured flower,
Which boys do flout us with; — but yet I love thee,
Thou giant rose, wrapped in a green surtout.

Doubtless in Eden thou didst blush as bright
As these, thy puny brethren; and thy breath
Sweetened the fragrance of her spicy air;
But now thou seemest like a bankrupt beau,
Stripped of his gaudy hues and essences,
And growing portly in his sober garments.

Is that a swan that rides upon the water?
O no, it is that other gentle bird,
Which is the patron of our noble calling.
I well remember, in my early years,
When these young hands first closed upon a goose;
I have a scar upon my thimble finger,
Which chronicles the hour of young ambition.
My father was a tailor, and his father,
And my sire's grandsire, all of them were tailors;
They had an ancient goose, — it was an heir-loom
From some remoter tailor of our race.
It happened I did see it on a time
When none was near, and I did deal with it,
And it did burn me, — oh, most fearfully!

It is a joy to straighten out one's limbs,
And leap elastic from the level counter,
Leaving the petty grievances of earth,

The breaking thread, the din of clashing shears,
And all the needles that do wound the spirit,
For such a pensive hour of soothing silence.
Kind Nature, shuffling in her loose undress,
Lays bare her shady bosom ; — I can feel
With all around me ; — I can hail the flowers
That sprig earth's mantle, — and yon quiet bird,
That rides the stream, is to me as a brother.
The vulgar know not all the hidden pockets,
Where Nature stows away her loveliness.
But this unnatural posture of the legs
Cramps my extended calves, and I must go
Where I can coil them in their wonted fashion.

THE DORCHESTER GIANT

THERE was a giant in time of old,
A mighty one was he;
He had a wife, but she was a scold,
So he kept her shut in his mammoth fold ·
And he had children three.

It happened to be an election day,
And the giants were choosing a kıng
The people were not democrats then,
They did not talk of the rights of men,
And all that sort of thing.

Then the giant took his children three
And fastened them in the pen;
The children roared; quoth the giant, "Be still!"
And Dorchester Heights and Milton Hill
Rolled back the sound again.

Then he brought them a pudding stuffed with plums,
As big as the State-House dome;
Quoth he, "There 's something for you to eat;
So stop your mouths with your 'lection treat,
And wait till your dad comes home."

So the giant pulled him a chestnut stout,
And whittled the boughs away;
The boys and their mother set up a shout,
Said he, "You 're in, and you can't get out,
Bellow as loud as you may."

Off he went, and he growled a tune
As he strode the fields along;
'T is said a buffalo fainted away,
And fell as cold as a lump of clay,
When he heard the giant's song.

But whether the story 's true or not,
It is not for me to show;
There 's many a thing that 's twice as queer
In somebody's lectures that we hear,
And those are true, you know.

* * * * *

What are those lone ones doing now,
The wife and the children sad?
O! they are in a terrible rout,
Screaming, and throwing their pudding about,
Acting as they were mad.

They flung it over to Roxbury hills,
They flung it over the plain,
And all over Milton and Dorchester too
Great lumps of pudding the giants threw;
They tumbled as thick as rain.

* * * * *

Giant and mammoth have passed away,
For ages have floated by;
The suet is hard as a marrow bone,
And every plum is turned to a stone,
But there the puddings lie.

And if, some pleasant afternoon,
You 'll ask me out to ride,
The whole of the story I will tell,
And you shall see where the puddings fell,
And pay for the punch beside.

TO THE PORTRAIT OF "A GENTLEMAN."

IN THE ATHENÆUM GALLERY.

It may be so, — perhaps thou hast
A warm and loving heart;
I will not blame thee for thy face,
Poor devil as thou art.

That thing, thou fondly deem'st a nose,
Unsightly though it be, —
In spite of all the cold world's scorn,
It may be much to thee.

Those eyes, — among thine elder friends
Perhaps they pass for blue; —
No matter, — if a man can see,
What more have eyes to do?

Thy mouth, — that fissure in thy face
By something like a chin, —
May be a very useful place
To put thy victual in.

I know thou hast a wife at home,
I know thou hast a child,
By that subdued, domestic smile
Upon thy features mild.

That wife sits fearless by thy side,
That cherub on thy knee;
They do not shudder at thy looks,
They do not shrink from thee.

Above thy mantel is a hook, —
A portrait once was there,
It was thine only ornament, —
Alas! that hook is bare.

She begged thee not to let it go,
She begged thee all in vain;
She wept, — and breathed a trembling prayer
To meet it safe again.

It was a bitter sight to see
That picture torn away;
It was a solemn thought to think
What all her friends would say!

And often in her calmer hours,
And in her happy dreams,
Upon its long-deserted hook
The absent portrait seems.

Thy wretched infant turns his head
In melancholy wise,
And looks to meet the placid stare
Of those unbending eyes.

I never saw thee, lovely one,—
Perchance I never may;
It is not often that we cross
Such people in our way;

But if we meet in distant years,
Or on some foreign shore,
Sure I can take my Bible oath,
I 've seen that face before.

TO THE PORTRAIT OF "A LADY."

IN THE ATHENÆUM GALLERY.

Well, Miss, I wonder where you live,
I wonder what 's your name,
I wonder how you came to be
In such a stylish frame;
Perhaps you were a favorite child,
Perhaps an only one;
Perhaps your friends were not aware
You had your portrait done!

Yet you must be a harmless soul;
I cannot think that Sin
Would care to throw his loaded dice,
With such a stake to win;
I cannot think you would provoke
The poet's wicked pen,
Or make young women bite their lips,
Or ruin fine young men.

Pray, did you ever hear, my love,
 Of boys that go about,
Who, for a very trifling sum,
 Will snip one's picture out?
I 'm not averse to red and white,
 But all things have their place,
I think a profile cut in black
 Would suit your style of face!

I love sweet features; I will own
 That I should like myself
To see my portrait on a wall,
 Or bust upon a shelf;
But nature sometimes makes one up
 Of such sad odds and ends,
It really might be quite as well
 Hushed up among one's friends!

THE COMET.

THE Comet! He is on his way,
And singing as he flies;
The whizzing planets shrink before
The spectre of the skies;
Ah! well may regal orbs burn blue,
And satellites turn pale,
Ten million cubic miles of head,
Ten billion leagues of tail!

On, on by whistling spheres of light,
He flashes and he flames;
He turns not to the left nor right,
He asks them not their names;
One spurn from his demoniac heel, —
Away, away they fly,
Where darkness might be bottled up
And sold for "Tyrian dye."

And what would happen to the land,
And how would look the sea,
If in the bearded devil's path
Our earth should chance to be?
Full hot and high the sea would boil,
Full red the forests gleam;
Methought I saw and heard it all
In a dyspeptic dream!

I saw a tutor take his tube
The Comet's course to spy;
I heard a scream,—the gathered rays
Had stewed the tutor's eye;
I saw a fort,—the soldiers all
Were armed with goggles green;
Pop cracked the guns! whiz flew the balls!
Bang went the magazine!

I saw a poet dip a scroll
Each moment in a tub,
I read upon the warping back,
"The Dream of Beelzebub";
He could not see his verses burn,
Although his brain was fried,
And ever and anon he bent
To wet them as they dried.

I saw the scalding pitch roll down
 The crackling, sweating pines,
And streams of smoke, like water-spouts
 Burst through the rumbling mines;
I asked the firemen why they made
 Such noise about the town;
They answered not,—but all the while
 The brakes went up and down.

I saw a roasting pullet sit
 Upon a baking egg;
I saw a cripple scorch his hand
 Extinguishing his leg;
I saw nine geese upon the wing
 Towards the frozen pole,
And every mother's gosling fell
 Crisped to a crackling coal.

I saw the ox that browsed the grass
 Writhe in the blistering rays,
The herbage in his shrinking jaws
 Was all a fiery blaze;
I saw huge fishes, boiled to rags,
 Bob through the bubbling brine;
And thoughts of supper crossed my soul;
 I had been rash at mine.

Strange sights! strange sounds! O fearful dream!
    Its memory haunts me still,
The steaming sea, the crimson glare,
    That wreathed each wooded hill;
Stranger! if through thy reeling brain
    Such midnight visions sweep,
Spare, spare, O spare thine evening meal,
    And sweet shall be thy sleep!

A NOONTIDE LYRIC.

The dinner-bell, the dinner-bell
  Is ringing loud and clear;
Through hill and plain, through street and lane,
  It echoes far and near;
From curtained hall, and whitewashed stall,
  Wherever men can hide,
Like bursting waves from ocean caves,
  They float upon the tide.

I smell the smell of roasted meat!
  I hear the hissing fry!
The beggars know where they can go,
  But where, O where shall I?
At twelve o'clock men took my hand,
  At two they only stare,
And eye me with a fearful look,
  As if I were a bear!

The poet lays his laurels down
And hastens to his greens;
The happy tailor quits his goose,
To riot on his beans;
The weary cobbler snaps his thread,
The printer leaves his pi;
His very devil hath a home,
But what, O what have I?

Methinks I hear an angel voice,
That softly seems to say;
"Pale stranger, all may yet be well,
Then wipe thy tears away;
Erect thy head, and cock thy hat,
And follow me afar,
And thou shalt have a jolly meal
And charge it at the bar."

I hear the voice! I go! I go!
Prepare your meat and wine!
They little heed their future need,
Who pay not when they dine.
Give me to-day the rosy bowl,
Give me one golden dream,—
To-morrow kick away the stool,
And dangle from the beam!

THE BALLAD OF THE OYSTERMAN.

It was a tall young oysterman lived by the river-side,
His shop was just upon the bank, his boat was on the tide;
The daughter of a fisherman, that was so straight and slim,
Lived over on the other bank, right opposite to him.

It was the pensive oysterman that saw a lovely maid,
Upon a moonlight evening, a sitting in the shade;
He saw her wave her handkerchief, as much as if to say,
"I'm wide awake, young oysterman, and all the folks away."

Then up arose the oysterman, and to himself said he,
"I guess I'll leave the skiff at home, for fear that folks should see;
I read it in the story-book, that, for to kiss his dear,
Leander swam the Hellespont,—and I will swim this here."

And he has leaped into the waves, and crossed the shining stream,
And he has clambered up the bank, all in the moonlight gleam;
O there were kisses sweet as dew, and words as soft as rain, —
But they have heard her father's step, and in he leaps again!

Out spoke the ancient fisherman, — "O what was that, my daughter?"
"'T was nothing but a pebble, sir, I threw into the water;"
"And what is that, pray tell me, love, that paddles off so fast?"
"It 's nothing but a porpoise, sir, that 's been a swimming past."

Out spoke the ancient fisherman, — "Now bring me my harpoon!
I 'll get into my fishing-boat, and fix the fellow soon;"
Down fell that pretty innocent, as falls a snow-white lamb,
Her hair drooped round her pallid cheeks, like sea-weed on a clam.

Alas for those two loving ones! she waked not from her
swound,
And he was taken with the cramp, and in the waves
was drowned;
But Fate has metamorphosed them, in pity of their woe,
And now they keep an oyster-shop for mermaids down
below.

THE MUSIC-GRINDERS.

THERE are three ways in which men take
One's money from his purse,
And very hard it is to tell
Which of the three is worse;
But all of them are bad enough
To make a body curse.

You 're riding out some pleasant day,
And counting up your gains;
A fellow jumps from out a bush,
And takes your horse's reins,
Another hints some words about
A bullet in your brains.

It 's hard to meet such pressing friends
In such a lonely spot;
It 's very hard to lose your cash,
But harder to be shot;
And so you take your wallet out,
Though you would rather not.

Perhaps you 're going out to dine, —
Some filthy creature begs
You 'll hear about the cannon-ball
That carried off his pegs,
And says it is a dreadful thing
For men to lose their legs.

He tells you of his starving wife,
His children to be fed,
Poor little, lovely innocents,
All clamorous for bread, —
And so you kindly help to put
A bachelor to bed.

You 're sitting on your window-seat
Beneath a cloudless moon;
You hear a sound, that seems to wear
The semblance of a tune,
As if a broken fife should strive
To drown a cracked bassoon.

And nearer, nearer still, the tide
Of music seems to come,
There 's something like a human voice,
And something like a drum;
You sit in speechless agony,
Until your ear is numb.

Poor "home, sweet home," should seem to be
A very dismal place;
Your "auld acquaintance," all at once,
Is altered in the face;
Their discords sting through Burns and Moore,
Like hedgehogs dressed in lace.

You think they are crusaders, sent
From some infernal clime,
To pluck the eyes of Sentiment,
And dock the tail of Rhyme,
To crack the voice of Melody,
And break the legs of Time.

But hark! the air again is still,
The music all is ground,
And silence, like a poultice, comes
To heal the blows of sound;
It cannot be, — it is, — it is, —
A hat is going round!

No! Pay the dentist when he leaves
A fracture in your jaw;
And pay the owner of the bear,
That stunned you with his paw,
And buy the lobster, that has had
Your knuckles in his claw;

But if you are a portly man,
    Put on your fiercest frown,
And talk about a constable
    To turn them out of town;
Then close your sentence with an oath,
    And shut the window down!

And if you are a slender man,
    Not big enough for that,
Or, if you cannot make a speech,
    Because you are a flat,
Go very quietly and drop
    A button in the hat!

THE TREADMILL SONG.

THE stars are rolling in the sky,
The earth rolls on below,
And we can feel the rattling wheel
Revolving as we go.
Then tread away, my gallant boys,
And make the axle fly;
Why should not wheels go round about,
Like planets in the sky?

Wake up, wake up, my duck-legged man,
And stir your solid pegs!
Arouse, arouse, my gawky friend,
And shake your spider legs;
What though you 're awkward at the trade,
There 's time enough to learn,—
So lean upon the rail, my lad,
And take another turn.

They 've built us up a noble wall,
To keep the vulgar out;
We 've nothing in the world to do,
But just to walk about;
So faster, now, you middle men,
And try to beat the ends, —
It 's pleasant work to ramble round
Among one's honest friends.

Here, tread upon the long man's toes,
He shan't be lazy here, —
And punch the little fellow's ribs,
And tweak that lubber's ear, —
He 's lost them both, — don't pull his hair,
Because he wears a scratch,
But poke him in the further eye,
That is n't in the patch.

Hark! fellows, there 's the supper-bell,
And so our work is done;
It 's pretty sport, — suppose we take
A round or two for fun!
If ever they should turn me out,
When I have better grown,
Now hang me, but I mean to have
A treadmill of my own!

THE SEPTEMBER GALE.

I 'M not a chicken; I have seen
Full many a chill September,
And though I was a youngster then,
That gale I well remember;
The day before, my kite-string snapped,
And I, my kite pursuing,
The wind whisked off my palm-leaf hat; —
For me two storms were brewing!

It came as quarrels sometimes do,
When married folks get clashing;
There was a heavy sigh or two,
Before the fire was flashing, —
A little stir among the clouds,
Before they rent asunder, —
A little rocking of the trees,
And then came on the thunder.

Lord! how the ponds and rivers boiled,
And how the shingles rattled!
And oaks were scattered on the ground
As if the Titans battled;
And all above was in a howl,
And all below a clatter, —
The earth was like a frying-pan,
Or some such hissing matter.

It chanced to be our washing-day,
And all our things were drying:
The storm came roaring through the lines,
And set them all a flying;
I saw the shirts and petticoats
Go riding off like witches;
I lost, ah! bitterly I wept, —
I lost my Sunday breeches!

I saw them straddling through the air,
Alas! too late to win them;
I saw them chase the clouds as if
The devil had been in them;
They were my darlings and my pride,
My boyhood's only riches, —
"Farewell, farewell," I faintly cried, —
"My breeches! O my breeches!"

That night I saw them in my dreams,
    How changed from what I knew them!
The dews had steeped their faded threads,
    The winds had whistled through them!
I saw the wide and ghastly rents
    Where demon claws had torn them;
A hole was in their amplest part,
    As if an imp had worn them.

I have had many happy years,
    And tailors kind and clever,
But those young pantaloons have gone
    Forever and forever!
And not till fate has cut the last
    Of all my earthly stitches,
This aching heart shall cease to mourn
    My loved, my long-lost breeches!

THE HEIGHT OF THE RIDICULOUS.

I wrote some lines once on a time
    In wondrous merry mood,
And thought, as usual, men would say
    They were exceeding good.

They were so queer, so very queer,
    I laughed as I would die;
Albeit, in the general way,
    A sober man am I.

I called my servant, and he came:
    How kind it was of him,
To mind a slender man like me,
    He of the mighty limb!

"These to the printer," I exclaimed,
    And, in my humorous way,
I added, (as a trifling jest,)
    "There 'll be the devil to pay."

He took the paper, and I watched,
And saw him peep within;
At the first line he read, his face
Was all upon the grin.

He read the next; the grin grew broad,
And shot from ear to ear;
He read the third; a chuckling noise
I now began to hear.

The fourth; he broke into a roar;
The fifth; his waistband split;
The sixth; he burst five buttons off,
And tumbled in a fit.

Ten days and nights, with sleepless eye,
I watched that wretched man,
And since, I never dare to write
As funny as I can.

THE HOT SEASON

THE folks, that on the first of May
    Wore winter-coats and hose,
Began to say, the first of June,
    "Good Lord! how hot it grows!"
At last two Fahrenheits blew up,
    And killed two children small,
And one barometer shot dead
    A tutor with its ball!

Now all day long the locusts sang
    Among the leafless trees;
Three new hotels warped inside out,
    The pumps could only wheeze;
And ripe old wine, that twenty years
    Had cobwebbed o'er in vain,
Came spouting through the rotten corks,
    Like Joly's best Champagne!

The Worcester locomotives did
    Their trip in half an hour;
The Lowell cars ran forty miles
    Before they checked the power;
Roll brimstone soon became a drug,
    And loco-focos fell;
All asked for ice, but everywhere
    Saltpetre was to sell.

Plump men of mornings ordered tights,
    But, ere the scorching noons,
Their candle-moulds had grown as loose
    As Cossack pantaloons!
The dogs ran mad,—men could not try
    If water they would choose;
A horse fell dead,—he only left
    Four red-hot, rusty shoes!

But soon the people could not bear
    The slightest hint of fire;
Allusions to caloric drew
    A flood of savage ire;
The leaves on heat were all torn out
    From every book at school,
And many blackguards kicked and caned,
    Because they said,—"Keep cool!"

The gas-light companies were mobbed,
The bakers all were shot,
The penny press began to talk
Of Lynching Doctor Nott;
And all about the warehouse steps
Were angry men in droves,
Crashing and splintering through the doors
To smash the patent stoves!

The abolition men and maids
Were tanned to such a hue,
You scarce could tell them from their friends,
Unless their eyes were blue;
And, when I left, society
Had burst its ancient guards,
And Brattle Street and Temple Place
Were interchanging cards!

POEMS

ADDED SINCE THE FIRST EDITION.

DEPARTED DAYS.

Yes, dear departed, cherished days,
Could Memory's hand restore
Your Morning light, your evening rays
From Time's gray urn once more,—
Then might this restless heart be still,
This straining eye might close,
And Hope her fainting pinions fold,
While the fair phantoms rose.

But, like a child in ocean's arms,
We strive against the stream,
Each moment farther from the shore
Where life's young fountains gleam;—
Each moment fainter wave the fields,
And wider rolls the sea;
The mist grows dark,—the sun goes down,—
Day breaks,—and where are we?

THE STEAMBOAT.

SEE how yon flaming herald treads
    The ridged and rolling waves,
As, crashing o'er their crested heads,
    She bows her surly slaves!
With foam before and fire behind,
    She rends the clinging sea,
That flies before the roaring wind,
    Beneath her hissing lee.

The morning spray, like sea-born flowers,
    With heaped and glistening bells,
Falls round her fast, in ringing showers,
    With every wave that swells,
And, burning o'er the midnight deep,
    In lurid fringes thrown,
The living gems of ocean sweep
    Along her flashing zone.

With clashing wheel, and lifting keel,
And smoking torch on high,
When winds are loud, and billows reel,
She thunders foaming by;
When seas are silent and serene,
With even beam she glides,
The sunshine glimmering through the green
That skirts her gleaming sides.

Now, like a wild nymph, far apart
She veils her shadowy form,
The beating of her restless heart
Still sounding through the storm;
Now answers, like a courtly dame,
The reddening surges o'er,
With flying scarf of spangled flame,
The Pharos of the shore.

To-night yon pilot shall not sleep,
Who trims his narrowed sail;
To-night yon frigate scarce shall keep
Her broad breast to the gale;
And many a foresail, scooped and strained,
Shall break from yard and stay,
Before this smoky wreath has stained
The rising mist of day.

Hark! hark! I hear yon whistling shroud,
    I see yon quivering mast;
The black throat of the hunted cloud
    Is panting forth the blast!
An hour, and, whirled like winnowing chaff,
    The giant surge shall fling
His tresses o'er yon pennon staff,
    White as the sea-bird's wing!

Yet rest, ye wanderers of the deep;
    Nor wind nor wave shall tire
Those fleshless arms, whose pulses leap
    With floods of living fire;
Sleep on,—and, when the morning light
    Streams o'er the shining bay,
O think of those for whom the night
    Shall never wake in day!

THE PARTING WORD.

I MUST leave thee, lady sweet!
Months shall waste before we meet;
Winds are fair, and sails are spread,
Anchors leave their ocean bed;
Ere this shining day grow dark,
Skies shall gird my shoreless bark;
Through thy tears, O lady mine,
Read thy lover's parting line.

When the first sad sun shall set,
Thou shalt tear thy locks of jet;
When the morning star shall rise,
Thou shalt wake with weeping eyes;
When the second sun goes down,
Thou more tranquil shalt be grown,
Taught too well that wild despair
Dims thine eyes, and spoils thy hair.

All the first unquiet week
Thou shalt wear a smileless cheek;
In the first month's second half
Thou shalt once attempt to laugh;
Then in Pickwick thou shalt dip,
Slightly puckering round the lip,
Till at last, in sorrow's spite,
Samuel makes thee laugh outright.

While the first seven mornings last,
Round thy chamber bolted fast,
Many a youth shall fume and pout,
"Hang the girl, she 's always out!"
While the second week goes round,
Vainly shall they ring and pound;
When the third week shall begin,
'Martha, let the creature in."

Now once more the flattering throng
Round thee flock with smile and song,
But thy lips, unweaned as yet,
Lisp, "O, how can I forget!"
Men and devils both contrive
Traps for catching girls alive;
Eve was duped, and Helen kissed,—
How, O how can you resist?

First be careful of your fan,
Trust it not to youth or man;
Love has filled a pirate's sail
Often with its perfumed gale.
Mind your kerchief most of all,
Fingers touch when kerchiefs fall;
Shorter ell than mercers clip,
Is the space from hand to lip.

Trust not such as talk in tropes,
Full of pistols, daggers, ropes;
All the hemp that Russia bears
Scarce would answer lovers' prayers,
Never thread was spun so fine,
Never spider stretched the line,
Would not hold the lovers true
That would really swing for you.

Fiercely some shall storm and swear,
Beating breasts in black despair;
Others murmur with a sigh,
You must melt or they will die;
Painted words on empty lies,
Grubs with wings like butterflies;
Let them die, and welcome, too;
Pray what better could they do?

Fare thee well, if years efface
From thy heart love's burning trace,
Keep, O keep that hallowed seat
From the tread of vulgar feet;
If the blue lips of the sea
Wait with icy kiss for me,
Let not thine forget the vow,
Sealed how often, Love, as now.

SONG,

WRITTEN FOR THE DINNER GIVEN TO CHARLES DICKENS,
BY THE YOUNG MEN OF BOSTON, FEB. 1, 1842.

The stars their early vigils keep,
The silent hours are near
When drooping eyes forget to weep, —
Yet still we linger here;
And what, — the passing churl may ask, —
Can claim such wondrous power,
That Toil forgets his wonted task,
And Love his promised hour?

The Irish harp no longer thrills,
Or breathes a fainter tone;
The clarion blast from Scotland's hills
Alas! no more is blown;
And Passion's burning lip bewails
Her Harold's wasted fire,
Still lingering o'er the dust that veils
The Lord of England's lyre.

But grieve not o'er its broken strings,
    Nor think its soul hath died,
While yet the lark at heaven's gate sings,
    As once o'er Avon's side ; —
While gentle summer sheds her bloom,
    And dewy blossoms wave,
Alike o'er Juliet's storied tomb
    And Nelly's nameless grave.

Thou glorious island of the sea !
    Though wide the wasting flood
That parts our distant land from thee,
    We claim thy generous blood ;
Nor o'er thy far horizon springs
    One hallowed star of fame,
But kindles, like an angel's wings,
    Our western skies in flame !

LINES

RECITED AT THE BERKSHIRE FESTIVAL.

Come back to your mother, ye children, for shame,
Who have wandered like truants, for riches or fame!
With a smile on her face, and a sprig in her cap,
She calls you to feast from her bountiful lap.

Come out from your alleys, your courts, and your lanes,
And breathe, like young eagles, the air of our plains;
Take a whiff from our fields, and your excellent wives
Will declare it 's all nonsense insuring your lives.

Come you of the law, who can talk, if you please,
Till the man in the moon will allow it 's a cheese,
And leave "the old lady, that never tells lies,"
To sleep with her handkerchief over her eyes.

Ye healers of men, for a moment decline
Your feats in the rhubarb and ipecac line;
While you shut up your turnpike, your neighbours can go
The old roundabout road, to the regions below.

You clerk, on whose ears are a couple of pens,
And whose head is an ant-hill of units and tens;
Though Plato denies you, we welcome you still
As a featherless biped, in spite of your quill.

Poor drudge of the city! how happy he feels,
With the burs on his legs, and the grass at his heels!
No *dodger* behind, his bandannas to share,
No constable grumbling, "You must n't walk there!"

In yonder green meadow, to memory dear,
He slaps a mosquito and brushes a tear;
The dewdrops hang round him on blossoms and shoots,
He breathes but one sigh for his youth and his boots.

There stands the old schoolhouse, hard by the old church;
That tree at its side had the flavor of birch;
O sweet were the days of his juvenile tricks,
Though the prairie of youth had so many "big licks,"

By the side of yon river he weeps and he slumps,
The boots fill with water, as if they were pumps;
Till, sated with rapture, he steals to his bed,
With a glow in his heart and a cold in his head.

'T is past,—he is dreaming,—I see him again;
The ledger returns as by legerdemain;
His neckcloth is damp with an easterly flaw,
And he holds in his fingers an omnibus straw.

He dreams the chill gust is a blossomy gale,
That the straw is a rose from his dear native vale;
And murmurs, unconscious of space and of time,
"A 1. Extra-super. Ah, is n't it PRIME!"

Oh what are the prizes we perish to win
To the first little "shiner" we caught with a pin!
No soil upon earth is so dear to our eyes
As the soil we first stirred in terrestrial pies!

Then come from all parties, and parts, to our feast;
Though not at the "Astor," we 'll give you at least
A bite at an apple, a seat on the grass,
And the best of old—water—at nothing a glass.

VERSES FOR AFTER-DINNER.

Φ. *B*. *K*. SOCIETY, 1844.

I WAS thinking last night, as I sat in the cars,
With the charmingest prospect of cinders and stars
Next Thursday is — bless me !—how hard it will be,
If that cannibal president calls upon me !

There is nothing on earth that he will not devour,
From a tutor in seed to a freshman in flower;
No sage is too gray, and no youth is too green,
And you can't be too plump, though you 're never toc
lean.

While others enlarge on the boiled and the roast,
He serves a raw clergyman up with a toast,
Or catches some doctor, quite tender and young,
And basely insists on a bit of his tongue.

Poor victim, prepared for his classical spit,
With a stuffing of praise, and a basting of wit,
You may twitch at your collar, and wrinkle your brow,
But you 're up on your legs, and you 're in for it now.

O think of your friends,—they are waiting to hear
Those jokes that are thought so remarkably queer;
And all the Jack Horners of metrical buns
Are prying and fingering to pick out the puns.

Those thoughts which, like chickens, will always thrive best
When reared by the heat of the natural nest,
Will perish if hatched from their embryo dream
In the mist and the glow of convivial steam.

O pardon me, then, if I meekly retire,
With a very small flash of ethereal fire;
No rubbing will kindle your Lucifer match,
If the *fiz* does not follow the primitive scratch.

Dear friends, who are listening so sweetly the while,
With your lips double reefed in a snug little smile,—
I leave you two fables, both drawn from the deep,—
The shells you can drop, but the pearls you may keep.

*   *   *   *   *

The fish called the FLOUNDER, perhaps you may know,
Has one side for use and another for show;
One side for the public, a delicate brown,
And one that is white, which he always keeps down.

A very young flounder, the flattest of flats,
(And they 're none of them thicker than opera hats,)
Was speaking more freely than charity taught
Of a friend and relation that just had been caught.

"My! what an exposure! just see what a sight!
I blush for my race,—he is showing his white!
Such spinning and wriggling,—why, what does he wish?
How painfully small to respectable fish!"

Then said an old SCULPIN,—"My freedom excuse,
But you 're playing the cobbler with holes in your shoes
Your brown side is up,—but just wait till you 're tried
And you 'll find that all flounders are white on one side.

* * * * *

There 's a slice near the PICKEREL's pectoral fins,
Where the *thorax* leaves off and the *venter* begins;
Which his brother, survivor of fish-hooks and lines,
Though fond of his family, never declines.

He loves his relations; he feels they 'll be missed;
But that one little tit-bit he cannot resist;
So your bait may be swallowed, no matter how fast,
For you catch your next fish with a piece of the last.

And thus, O survivor, whose merciless fate
Is to take the next hook with the president's bait,
You are lost while you snatch from the end of his line
The morsel he rent from this bosom of mine!

SONG,

FOR A TEMPERANCE DINNER TO WHICH LADIES WERE INVITED.
(NEW YORK MERCANTILE LIBRARY ASSOCIATION, NOV. 1842.)

A HEALTH to dear woman! She bids us untwine,
From the cup it encircles, the fast-clinging vine;
But her cheek in its crystal with pleasure will glow,
And mirror its bloom in the bright wave below.

A health to sweet woman! The days are no more
When she watched for her lord till the revel was o'er,
And smoothed the white pillow, and blushed when he came,
As she pressed her cold lips on his forehead of flame.

Alas for the loved one! too spotless and fair
The joys of his banquet to chasten and share;
Her eye lost its light that his goblet might shine,
And the rose of her cheek was dissolved in his wine.

Joy smiles in the fountain, health flows in the rills,
As their ribands of silver unwind from the hills;
They breathe not the mist of the bacchanal's dream,
But the lilies of innocence float on their stream.

Then a health and a welcome to woman once more!
She brings us a passport that laughs at our door;
It is written on crimson,—its letters are pearls,—
It is countersigned *Nature*.——So, room for the Girls!

THE ONLY DAUGHTER.

(ILLUSTRATION OF A PICTURE.)

THEY bid me strike the idle strings,
  As if my summer days
Had shaken sunbeams from their wings,
  To warm my autumn lays;
They bring to me their painted urn,
  As if it were not time
To lift my gauntlet and to spurn
  The lists of boyish rhyme;
And, were it not that I have still
  Some weakness in my heart
That clings around my stronger will
  And pleads for gentler art,
Perchance I had not turned away
  The thoughts grown tame with toil,
To cheat this lone and pallid ray,
  That wastes the midnight oil.

Alas! with every year I feel
   Some roses leave my brow;
Too young for wisdom's tardy seal,
   Too old for garlands now;
Yet, while the dewy breath of spring
   Steals o'er the tingling air,
And spreads and fans each emerald wing
   The forest soon shall wear,
How bright the opening year would seem,
   Had I one look like thine,
To meet me when the morning beam
   Unseals these lids of mine!
Too long I bear this lonely lot,
   That bids my heart run wild
To press the lips that love me not,
   To clasp the stranger's child.

How oft beyond the dashing seas,
   Amidst those royal bowers,
Where danced the lilacs in the breeze,
   And swung the chestnut flowers,
I wandered like a wearied slave
   Whose morning task is done,
To watch the little hands that gave
   Their whiteness to the sun;

To revel in the bright young eyes,
  Whose lustre sparkled through
The sable fringe of southern skies,
  Or gleamed in Saxon blue!
How oft I heard another's name
  Called in some truant's tone;
Sweet accents! which I longed to claim,
  To learn and lisp my own!

Too soon the gentle hands, that pressed
  The ringlets of the child,
Are folded on the faithful breast
  Where first he breathed and smiled;
Too oft the clinging arms untwine,
  The melting lips forget,
And darkness veils the bridal shrine
  Where wreaths and torches met;
If Heaven but leaves a single thread
  Of Hope's dissolving chain,
Even when her parting plumes are spread,
  It bids them fold again;
The cradle rocks beside the tomb;
  The cheek now changed and chill,
Smiles on us in the morning bloom
  Of one that loves us still.

Sweet image! I have done thee wrong
  To claim this destined lay;
The leaf that asked an idle song
  Must bear my tears away.
Yet, in thy memory shouldst thou keep
  This else forgotten strain,
Till years have taught thine eyes to weep
  And flattery's voice is vain;
O then, thou fledgling of the nest,
  Like the long-wandering dove,
Thy weary heart may faint for rest,
  As mine, on changeless love;
And, while these sculptured lines retrace
  The hours now dancing by,
This vision of thy girlish grace
  May cost theè, too, a sigh.

LEXINGTON.

Slowly the mist o'er the meadow was creeping,
  Bright on the dewy buds glistened the sun,
When from his couch, while his children were sleeping,
  Rose the bold rebel and shouldered his gun.
      Waving her golden veil
      Over the silent dale,
Blithe looked the morning on cottage and spire;
      Hushed was his parting sigh,
      While from his noble eye
Flashed the last sparkle of liberty's fire.

On the smooth green where the fresh leaf is springing
  Calmly the first-born of glory have met;
Hark! the death-volley around them is ringing!
  Look! with their life-blood the young grass is wet!

Faint is the feeble breath,
Murmuring low in death,
"Tell to our sons how their fathers have died;"
Nerveless the iron hand,
Raised for its native land,
Lies by the weapon that gleams at its side.

Over the hill-sides the wild knell is tolling,
From their far hamlets the yeomanry come;
As through the storm-clouds the thunder-burst rolling,
Circles the beat of the mustering drum.
Fast on the soldier's path
Darken the waves of wrath,
Long have they gathered and loud shall they fall;
Red glares the musket's flash,
Sharp rings the rifle's crash,
Blazing and clanging from thicket and wall.

Gaily the plume of the horseman was dancing,
Never to shadow his cold brow again;
Proudly at morning the war-steed was prancing,
Reeking and panting he droops on the rein;
Pale is the lip of scorn,
Voiceless the trumpet horn,
Torn is the silken-fringed red cross on high;

Many a belted breast
Low on the turf shall rest,
Ere the dark hunters the herd have past by.

Snow-girdled crags where the hoarse wind is raving,
Rocks where the weary floods murmur and wail,
Wilds where the fern by the furrow is waving,
Reeled with the echoes that rode on the gale;
Far as the tempest thrills
Over the darkened hills,
Far as the sunshine streams over the plain,
Roused by the tyrant band,
Woke all the mighty land,
Girded for battle, from mountain to main.

Green be the graves where her martyrs are lying!
Shroudless and tombless they sunk to their rest,—
While o'er their ashes the starry fold flying
Wraps the proud eagle they roused from his nest.
Borne on her northern pine,
Long o'er the foaming brine
Spread her broad banner to storm and to sun;
Heaven keep her ever free,
Wide as o'er land and sea
Floats the fair emblem her heroes have won.

THE ISLAND HUNTING SONG.

No more the summer floweret charms,
    The leaves will soon be sere,
And Autumn folds his jewelled arms
    Around the dying year;
So, ere the waning seasons claim
    Our leafless groves a while,
With golden wine and glowing flame
    We 'll crown our lonely isle.

Once more the merry voices sound
    Within the antlered hall,
And long and loud the baying hounds
    Return the hunter's call;
And through the woods, and o'er the hill,
    And far along the bay,
The driver's horn is sounding shrill,—
    Up, sportsmen, and away!

No bars of steel, or walls of stone,
Our little empire bound,
But, circling with his azure zone,
The sea runs foaming round;
The whitening wave, the purpled skies,
The blue and lifted shore,
Braid with their dim and blending dyes
Our wide horizon o'er.

And who will leave the grave debate
That shakes the smoky town,
To rule amid our island-state,
And wear our oak-leaf crown?
And who will be a while content
To hunt our woodland game,
And leave the vulgar pack that scent
The reeking track of fame?

Ah, who that shares in toils like these
Will sigh not to prolong
Our days beneath the broad-leaved trees,
Our nights of mirth and song?
Then leave the dust of noisy streets,
Ye outlaws of the wood,
And follow through his green retreats
Your noble Robin Hood

QUESTIONS AND ANSWERS.

WHERE, O where are the visions of morning,
Fresh as the dews of our prime?
Gone, like tenants that quit without warning,
Down the back entry of time.

Where, O where are life's lilies and roses,
Nursed in the golden dawn's smile?
Dead as the bulrushes round little Moses,
On the old banks of the Nile.

Where are the Marys, and Anns, and Elizas,
Loving and lovely of yore?
Look in the columns of old Advertisers,—
Married and dead by the score.

Where the gray colts and the ten-year-old fillies,
Saturday's triumph and joy?
Gone like our friend πόδας ὠκυς Achilles,
Homer's ferocious old boy.

Die-away dreams of ecstatic emotion,
Hopes like young eagles at play,
Vows of unheard of and endless devotion,
How ye have faded away!

Yet, though the ebbing of Time's mighty river
Leave our young blossoms to die,
Let him roll smooth in his current for ever,
Till the last pebble is dry.

A SONG

FOR THE CENTENNIAL CELEBRATION OF HARVARD COLLEGE, 1836

When the Puritans came over,
    Our hills and swamps to clear,
The woods were full of catamounts,
    And Indians red as deer,
With tomahawks and scalping-knives,
    That make folks' heads look queer;—
O the ship from England used to bring
    A hundred wigs a year!

The crows came cawing through the air
    To pluck the pilgrims' corn,
The bears came snuffing round the door
    Whene'er a babe was born,
The rattlesnakes were bigger round
    Than the butt of the old ram's horn
The deacon blew at meeting time
    On every "Sabbath" morn.

But soon they knocked the wigwams down,
And pine-tree trunk and limb
Began to sprout among the leaves
In shape of steeples slim;
And out the little wharves were stretched
Along the ocean's rim,
And up the little schoolhouse shot
To keep the boys in trim.

And, when at length the College rose,
The sachem cocked his eye
At every tutor's meagre ribs
Whose coat-tails whistled by;
But, when the Greek and Hebrew words
Came tumbling from their jaws,
The copper-colored children all
Ran screaming to the squaws.

And who was on the Catalogue
When college was begun?
Two nephews of the President,
And *the* Professor's son,
(They turned a little Indian by,
As brown as any bun;)
Lord! how the seniors knocked about
The freshman class of one!

They had not then the dainty things
    That commons now afford,
But *succotash* and *homony*
    Were smoking on the board;
They did not rattle round in gigs,
    Or dash in long-tail blues,
But always on Commencement days
    The tutors blacked their shoes.

God bless the ancient Puritans!
    Their lot was hard enough;
But honest hearts make iron arms,
    And tender maids are tough;
So love and faith have formed and fed
    Our true-born Yankee stuff,
And keep the kernel in the shell
    The British found so rough!

TERPSICHORE.*

In narrowest girdle, O reluctant Muse,
In closest frock and Cinderella shoes,
Bound to the foot-lights for thy brief display,
One zephyr step, and then dissolve away!

Short is the space that gods and men can spare
To Song's twin brother when she is not there.
Let others water every lusty line,
As Homer's heroes did their purple wine;
Pierian revellers! Know in strains like these
The native juice, the real honest squeeze, —
Strains that, diluted to the twentieth power,
In yon grave temple† might have filled an hour.

---

* Read at the Annual Dinner of the *Φ. B. K.* Society, at Cambridge, August 24, 1843.

† The Annual Poem is always delivered in the neighbouring church.

Small room for Fancy's many-chorded lyre,
For Wit's bright rockets with their trains of fire,
For Pathos, struggling vainly to surprise
The iron tutor's tear-denying eyes,
For Mirth, whose finger with delusive wile
Turns the grim key of many a rusty smile,
For Satire, emptying his corrosive flood
On hissing Folly's gas-exhaling brood,
The pun, the fun, the moral and the joke,
The hit, the thrust, the pugilistic poke,—
Small space for these, so pressed by niggard Time,
Like that false matron, known to nursery rhyme,—
Insidious Morey,—scarce her tale begun,
Ere listening infants weep the story done.

O had we room to rip the mighty bags
That Time, the harlequin, has stuffed with rags!
Grant us one moment to unloose the strings,
While the old gray-beard shuts his leather wings.
But what a heap of motley trash appears
Crammed in the bundles of successive years!
As the lost rustic on some festal day
Stares through the concourse in its vast array,—
Where in one cake a throng of faces runs,
All stuck together like a sheet of buns,—

And throws the bait of some unheeded name,
Or shoots a wink with most uncertain aim,
So roams my vision, wandering over all,
And strives to choose, but knows not where to fall.

Skins of flayed authors,—husks of dead reviews,—
The turn-coat's clothes,—the office-seeker's shoes,—
Scraps from cold feasts, where conversation runs
Through mouldy toasts to oxydated puns,
And grating songs a listening crowd endures,
Rasped from the throats of bellowing amateurs;—
Sermons, whose writers played such dangerous tricks
Their own heresiarchs called them heretics,
(Strange that one term such distant poles should link,
The Priestleyan's copper and the Puseyan's zinc;)—
Poems that shuffle with superfluous legs
A blindfold minuet over addled eggs,
Where all the syllables that end in éd,
Like old dragoons, have cuts across the head;—
Essays so dark Champollion might despair
To guess what mummy of a thought was there,
Where our poor English, striped with foreign phrase,
Looks like a Zebra in a parson's chaise;—
Lectures that cut our dinners down to roots,
Or prove (by monkeys) men should stick to fruits;

Delusive error,—as at trifling charge
Professor Gripes will certify at large;—
Mesmeric pamphlets, which to facts appeal,
Each fact as slippery as a fresh-caught eel;—
And figured heads, whose hieroglyphs invite
To wandering knaves that discount fools at sight;—
Such things as these, with heaps of unpaid bills,
And candy puffs and homœopathic pills,
And ancient bell-crowns with contracted rim,
And bonnets hideous with expanded brim,
And coats whose memory turns the sartor pale,
Their sequels tapering like a lizard's tail;—
How might we spread them to the smiling day,
And toss them, fluttering like the new-mown hay,
To laughter's light or sorrow's pitying shower,
Were these brief minutes lengthened to an hour.

The narrow moments fit like Sunday shoes,
How vast the heap, how quickly must we choose;
A few small scraps from out his mountain mass
We snatch in haste, and let the vagrant pass.

This shrunken CRUST that Cerberus could not bite,
Stamped (in one corner) "Pickwick copyright,"

Kneaded by youngsters, raised by flattery's yeast,
Was once a loaf, and helped to make a feast.
He for whose sake the glittering show appears
Has sown the world with laughter and with tears,
And they whose welcome wets the bumper's brim
Have wit and wisdom,—for they all quote him.
So, many a tongue the evening hour prolongs
With spangled speeches,—let alone the songs,—
Statesmen grow merry, lean attorneys laugh,
And weak teetotals warm to half and half,
And beardless Tullys, new to festive scenes,
Cut their first crop of youth's precocious greens,
And wits stand ready for impromptu claps,
With loaded barrels and percussion caps,
And Pathos, cantering through the minor keys,
Waves all her onions to the trembling breeze;
While the great Feasted views with silent glee
His scattered limbs in Yankee fricassee.

Sweet is the scene where genial friendship plays
The pleasing game of interchanging praise;
Self-love, grimalkin of the human heart,
Is ever pliant to the master's art;
Soothed with a word, she peacefully withdraws
And sheathes in velvet her obnoxious claws.

And thrills the hand that smooths her glossy fur
With the light tremor of her grateful purr.

But what sad music fills the quiet hall,
If on her back a feline rival fall;
And O, what noises shake the tranquil house,
If old Self-interest cheats her of a mouse!

Thou, O my country, hast thy foolish ways,
Too apt to purr at every stranger's praise;
But, if the stranger touch thy modes or laws,
Off goes the velvet and out come the claws!
And thou, Illustrious! but too poorly paid
In toasts from Pickwick for thy great crusade,
Though, while the echoes labored with thy name,
The public trap denied thy little game,
Let other lips our jealous laws revile,—
The marble Talfourd or the rude Carlyle,—
But on thy lids, that Heaven forbids to close
Where'er the light of kindly nature glows,
Let not the dollars that a churl denies
Weigh like the shillings on a dead man's eyes!
Or, if thou wilt, be more discreetly blind,
Nor ask to see all wide extremes combined.

Not in our wastes the dainty blossoms smile,
That crowd the gardens of thy scanty isle.
There white-cheeked Luxury weaves a thousand charms;—
Here sun-browned Labor swings his naked arms.
Long are the furrows he must trace between
The ocean's azure and the prairie's green;
Full many a blank his destined realm displays,
Yet see the promise of his riper days:
Far through yon depths the panting engine moves,
His chariots ringing in their steel-shod grooves;
And Erie's naiad flings her diamond wave
O'er the wild sea-nymph in her distant cave!
While tasks like these employ his anxious hours,
What if his corn-fields are not edged with flowers?
Though bright as silver the meridian beams
Shine through the crystal of thine English streams,
Turbid and dark the mighty wave is whirled
That drains our Andes and divides a world!

But lo! a PARCHMENT! Surely it would seem
The sculptured impress speaks of power supreme;
Some grave design the solemn page must claim
That shows so broadly an emblazoned name;
A sovereign's promise! Look, the lines afford
All Honor gives when Caution asks his word;

There sacred Faith has laid her snow-white hands,
And awful Justice knit her iron bands;
Yet every leaf is stained with treachery's dye,
And every letter crusted with a lie.
Alas! no treason has degraded yet
The Arab's salt, the Indian's calumet;
A simple rite, that bears the wanderer's pledge,
Blunts the keen shaft and turns the dagger's edge;—
While jockeying senates stop to sign and seal,
And freeborn statesmen legislate to steal.
Rise, Europe, tottering with thine Atlas load,
Turn thy proud eye to Freedom's blest abode,
And round her forehead, wreathed with heavenly flame,
Bind the dark garland of her daughter's shame!
Ye ocean clouds, that wrap the angry blast,
Coil her stained ensign round its haughty mast,
Or tear the fold that wears so foul a scar,
And drive a bolt through every blackened star!

Once more,—once only,—we must stop so soon,—
What have we here? A GERMAN-SILVER SPOON;
A cheap utensil, which we often see
Used by the dabblers in æsthetic tea;
Of slender fabric, somewhat light and thin,
Made of mixed metal, chiefly lead and tin;

The bowl is shallow, and the handle small
Marked in large letters with the name JEAN PAUL.
Small as it is, its powers are passing strange,
For all who use it show a wondrous change;
And first, a fact to make the barbers stare,
It beats Macassar for the growth of hair;
See those small youngsters whose expansive ears
Maternal kindness grazed with frequent shears;
Each bristling crop a dangling mass becomes,
And all the spoonies turn to Absaloms!
Nor this alone its magic power displays,
It alters strangely all their works and ways;
With uncouth words they tire their tender lungs,
The same bald phrases on their hundred tongues;
"Ever" "The Ages" in their page appear,
"Alway" the bedlamite is called a "Seer";
On every leaf the "earnest" sage may scan,
Portentous bore! their "many-sided" man,—
A weak eclectic, groping vague and dim,
Whose every angle is a half-starved whim,
Blind as a mole and curious as a lynx,
Who rides a beetle, which he calls a "Sphinx."
And O what questions asked in club-foot rhyme
Of Earth the tongueless and the deaf-mute Time!

Here babbling "Insight" shouts in Nature's ears
His last conundrum on the orbs and spheres;
There Self-inspection sucks its little thumb,
With "Whence am I?" and "Wherefore did I come?"
Deluded infants! will they ever know
Some doubts must darken o'er the world below,
Though all the Platos of the nursery trail
Their "clouds of glory" at the go-cart's tail?
O might these couplets their attention claim,
That gain their author the Philistine's name;
(A stubborn race, that, spurning foreign law,
Was much belabored with an ass's jaw!)

Melodious Laura! From the sad retreats
That hold thee, smothered with excess of sweets,
Shade of a shadow, spectre of a dream,
Glance thy wan eye across the Stygian stream!
The slip-shod dreamer treads thy fragrant halls,
The sophist's cobwebs hang thy roseate walls,
And o'er the crotchets of thy jingling tunes
The bard of mystery scrawls his crooked "runes."
Yes, thou art gone, with all the tuneful hordes
That candied thoughts in amber-colored words,
And in the precincts of thy late abodes
The clattering verse-wright hammers Orphic odes.

Thou, soft as zephyr, wast content to fly
On the gilt pinions of a balmy sigh;
He, vast as Phœbus on his burning wheels,
Would stride through ether at Orion's heels;
Thy emblem, Laura, was a perfume-jar,
And thine, young Orpheus, is a pewter star;
The balance trembles,—be its verdict told
When the new jargon slumbers with the old!

Cease, playful goddess! From thine airy bound
Drop like a feather softly to the ground;
This light bolero grows a ticklish dance,
And there is mischief in thy kindling glance.
To-morrow bids thee, with rebuking frown,
Change thy gauze tunic for a home-made gown,
Too blest by fortune, if the passing day
Adorn thy bosom with its frail bouquet,
But O still happier if the next forgets
Thy daring steps and dangerous pirouettes!

URANIA:

A RHYMED LESSON.*

Yes, dear Enchantress,—wandering far and long,
In realms unperfumed by the breath of song,
Where flowers ill-flavored shed their sweets around,
And bitterest roots invade the ungenial ground,
Whose gems are crystals from the Epsom mine,
Whose vineyards flow with antimonial wine,
Whose gates admit no mirthful feature in,
Save one gaunt mocker, the Sardonic grin,
Whose pangs are real, not the woes of rhyme
That blue-eyed misses warble out of time;—
Truant, not recreant to thy sacred claim,
Older by reckoning, but in heart the same,
Freed for a moment from the chains of toil,
I tread once more thy consecrated soil;
Here at thy feet my old allegiance own,
Thy subject still, and loyal to thy throne!

---

* This poem was delivered before the Boston Mercantile Library Association, October 14, 1846.

My dazzled glance explores the crowded hall,
Alas, how vain to hope the smiles of all!
I know my audience. All the gay and young
Love the light antics of a playful tongue;
And these, remembering some expansive line
My lips let loose among the nuts and wine,
Are all impatience till the opening pun
Proclaim the witty shamfight is begun.
Two fifths at least, if not the total half,
Have come infuriate for an earthquake laugh;
I know full well what alderman has tied
His red bandanna tight about his side;
I see the mother, who, aware that boys
Perform their laughter with superfluous noise,
Beside her kerchief, brought an extra one
To stop the explosions of her bursting son;
I know a tailor, once a friend of mine,
Expects great doings in the button line;—
For mirth's concussions rip the outward case,
And plant the stitches in a tenderer place.
I know my audience;—these shall have their due;
A smile awaits them ere my song is through!

I know myself. Not servile for applause,
My Muse permits no deprecating clause;

Modest or vain, she will not be denied
One bold confession, due to honest pride;
And well she knows, the drooping veil of song
Shall save her boldness from the caviller's wrong.
Her sweeter voice the Heavenly Maid imparts
To tell the secrets of our aching hearts;
For this, a suppliant, captive, prostrate, bound,
She kneels imploring at the feet of sound;
For this, convulsed in thought's maternal pains,
She loads her arms with rhyme's resounding chains;
Faint though the music of her fetters be,
It lends one charm;—her lips are ever free!

Think not I come, in manhood's fiery noon,
To steal his laurels from the stage buffoon;
His sword of lath the harlequin may wield;
Behold the star upon my lifted shield!
Though the just critic pass my humble name,
And sweeter lips have drained the cup of fame,
While my gay stanza pleased the banquet's lords,
The soul within was tuned to deeper chords!
Say, shall my arms, in other conflicts taught
To swing aloft the ponderous mace of thought,
Lift, in obedience to a school-girl's law,
Mirth's tinsel wand or laughter's tickling straw?

Say, shall I wound with satire's rankling spear
The pure, warm hearts that bid me welcome here?
No! while I wander through the land of dreams
To strive with great and play with trifling themes,
Let some kind meaning fill the varied line;
You have your judgment; will you trust to mine?

BETWEEN two breaths what crowded mysteries lie —
The first short gasp, the last and long-drawn sigh!
Like phantoms painted on the magic slide,
Forth from the darkness of the past we glide,
As living shadows for a moment seen
In airy pageant on the eternal screen,
Traced by a ray from one unchanging flame,
Then seek the dust and stillness whence we came.

But whence and why, our trembling souls inquire,
Caught these dim visions their awakening fire?
O who forgets when first the piercing thought
Through childhood's musings found its way unsought.
I AM;—I LIVE. The mystery and the fear
When the dread question—WHAT HAS BROUGHT ME HERE?

Burst through life's twilight, as before the sun
Roll the deep thunders of the morning gun!

Are angel faces, silent and serene,
Bent on the conflicts of this little scene,
Whose dreamlike efforts, whose unreal strife,
Are but the preludes to a larger life?

Or does life's summer see the end of all,
These leaves of being mouldering as they fall,
As the old poet vaguely used to deem,
As WESLEY questioned in his youthful dream?[1]
O could such mockery reach our souls indeed,
Give back the Pharaohs' or the Athenian's creed;
Better than this a Heaven of man's device,—
The Indian's sports, the Moslem's paradise!

Or is our being's only end and aim
To add new glories to our Maker's name,
As the poor insect, shrivelling in the blaze,
Lends a faint sparkle to its streaming rays?
Does earth send upwards to the Eternal's ear
The mingled discords of her jarring sphere
To swell his anthem, while Creation rings
With notes of anguish from its shattered strings?

Is it for this the immortal Artist means
These conscious, throbbing, agonized machines?

Dark is the soul whose sullen creed can bind
In chains like these the all-embracing Mind;
No! two-faced bigot, thou dost ill reprove
The sensual, selfish, yet benignant Jove,
And praise a tyrant throned in lonely pride,
Who loves himself, and cares for nought beside;
Who gave thee, summoned from primeval night,
A thousand laws, and not a single right;
A heart to feel and quivering nerves to thrill,
The sense of wrong, the death-defying will;
Who girt thy senses with this goodly frame,
Its earthly glories and its orbs of flame,
Not for thyself, unworthy of a thought,
Poor helpless victim of a life unsought,
But all for him, unchanging and supreme,
The heartless centre of thy frozen scheme!

Trust not the teacher with his lying scroll,
Who tears the charter of thy shuddering soul;
The God of love, who gave the breath that warms
All living dust in all its varied forms,

Asks not the tribute of a world like this
To fill the measure of his perfect bliss.
Though winged with life through all its radiant shores,
Creation flowed with unexhausted stores
Cherub and seraph had not yet enjoyed;
For this he called thee from the quickening void!
Nor this alone; a larger gift was thine,
A mightier purpose swelled his vast design;
Thought,—conscience,—will,—to make them all thine
own,
He rent a pillar from the eternal throne!

Made in his image, thou must nobly dare
The thorny crown of sovereignty to share.
With eye uplifted it is thine to view,
From thine own centre, Heaven's o'erarching blue;
So round thy heart a beaming circle lies
No fiend can blot, no hypocrite disguise;
From all its orbs one cheering voice is heard,
Full to thine ear it bears the Father's word,
Now, as in Eden where his first-born trod:
"Seek thine own welfare, true to man and God!"
Think not too meanly of thy low estate;
Thou hast a choice; to choose is to create!

Remember whose the sacred lips that tell,
Angels approve thee when thy choice is well;
Remember, One, a judge of righteous men,
Swore to spare Sodom if she held but ten!
Use well the freedom which thy Master gave,
(Think'st thou that Heaven can tolerate a slave?)
And He who made thee to be just and true
Will bless thee, love thee, — ay, respect thee too!

Nature has placed thee on a changeful tide,
To breast its waves, but not without a guide;
Yet, as the needle will forget its aim,
Jarred by the fury of the electric flame,
As the true current it will falsely feel,
Warped from its axis by a freight of steel;
So will thy CONSCIENCE lose its balanced truth,
If passion's lightning fall upon thy youth;
So the pure effluence quit its sacred hold,
Girt round too deeply with magnetic gold.
Go to yon tower, where busy science plies
Her vast antennæ, feeling through the skies;
That little vernier on whose slender lines
The midnight taper trembles as it shines,
A silent index, tracks the planets' march
In all their wanderings through the ethereal arch,

Tells through the mist where dazzled Mercury burns,
And marks the spot where Uranus returns.
  So, till by wrong or negligence effaced,
The living index which thy Maker traced
Repeats the line each starry Virtue draws
Through the wide circuit of creation's laws;
Still tracks unchanged the everlasting ray
Where the dark shadows of temptation stray;
But, once defaced, forgets the orbs of light,
And leaves thee wandering o'er the expanse of night!

  "What is thy creed?" a hundred lips inquire;
"Thou seekest God beneath what Christian spire?"
Nor ask they idly, for uncounted lies
Float upward on the smoke of sacrifice;
When man's first incense rose above the plain,
Of earth's two altars one was built by Cain!
  Uncursed by doubt, our earliest creed we take;
We love the precepts for the teacher's sake;
The simple lessons which the nursery taught
Fell soft and stainless on the buds of thought,
And the full blossom owes its fairest hue
To those sweet tear-drops of affection's dew.
  Too oft the light that led our earlier hours
Fades with the perfume of our cradle flowers;

The clear, cold question chills to frozen doubt;
Tired of beliefs, we dread to live without;
O then, if reason waver at thy side,
Let humbler Memory be thy gentle guide;
Go to thy birth-place, and, if faith was there,
Repeat thy father's creed, thy mother's prayer!

Faith loves to lean on Time's destroying arm,
And age, like distance, lends a double charm;
In dim cathedrals, dark with vaulted gloom,
What holy awe invests the saintly tomb!
There pride will bow, and anxious care expand,
And creeping avarice come with open hand;
The gay can weep, the impious can adore,
From morn's first glimmerings on the chancel floor
Till dying sunset sheds his crimson stains
Through the faint halos of the irised panes.

Yet there are graves, whose rudely-shapen sod
Bears the fresh footprints where the sexton trod;
Graves where the verdure has not dared to shoot,
Where the chance wild-flower has not fixed its root,
Whose slumbering tenants, dead without a name,
The eternal record shall at length proclaim
Pure as the holiest in the long array
Of hooded, mitred, or tiaraed clay!

Come, seek the air; some pictures we may gain
Whose passing shadows shall not be in vain;
Not from the scenes that crowd the stranger's soil,
Not from our own amidst the stir of toil,
But when the Sabbath brings its kind release,
And Care lies slumbering on the lap of Peace.

The air is hushed; the street is holy ground;
Hark! The sweet bells renew their welcome sound;
As one by one awakes each silent tongue,
It tells the turret whence its voice is flung.[2]

The Chapel, last of sublunary things
That shocks our echoes with the name of Kings,
Whose bell, just glistening from the font and forge
Rolled its proud requiem for the second George,
Solemn and swelling, as of old it rang,
Flings to the wind its deep, sonorous clang; —
The simpler pile, that, mindful of the hour
When Howe's artillery shook its half-built tower,
Wears on its bosom, as a bride might do,
The iron breastpin which the "Rebels" threw,
Wakes the sharp echoes with the quivering thrill
Of keen vibrations, tremulous and shrill; —
Aloft, suspended in the morning's fire,
Crash the vast cymbals from the Southern spire; —

The Giant, standing by the elm-clad green,
His white lance lifted o'er the silent scene,
Whirling in air his brazen goblet round,
Swings from its brim the swollen floods of sound; —
While, sad with memories of the olden time,
The Northern Minstrel pours her tender chime,
Faint, single tones, that spell their ancient song,
But tears still follow as they breathe along.

Child of the soil, whom fortune sends to range
Where man and nature, faith and customs change,
Borne in thy memory, each familiar tone
Mourns on the winds that sigh in every zone.
When Ceylon sweeps thee with her perfumed breeze
Through the warm billows of the Indian seas;
When, — ship and shadow blended both in one, —
Flames o'er thy mast the equatorial sun,
From sparkling midnight to refulgent noon
Thy canvas swelling with the still monsoon;
When through thy shrouds the wild tornado sings,
And thy poor seabird folds her tattered wings,
Oft will delusion o'er thy senses steal,
And airy echoes ring the Sabbath peal!
Then, dim with grateful tears, in long array
Rise the fair town, the island-studded bay,

Home, with its smiling board, its cheering fire,
The half-choked welcome of the expecting sire,
The mother's kiss, and, still if aught remain,
Our whispering hearts shall aid the silent strain.—
Ah, let the dreamer o'er the taffrail lean
To muse unheeded, and to weep unseen;
Fear not the tropic's dews, the evening's chills,
His heart lies warm among his triple hills!

Turned from her path by this deceitful gleam,
My wayward fancy half forgets her theme;
See through the streets that slumbered in repose
The living current of devotion flows;
Its varied forms in one harmonious band,
Age leading childhood by its dimpled hand,
Want, in the robe whose faded edges fall
To tell of rags beneath the tartan shawl,
And wealth, in silks that, fluttering to appear,
Lift the deep borders of the proud cashmere.

See, but glance briefly, sorrow-worn and pale,
Those sunken cheeks beneath the widow's veil;
Alone she wanders where with *him* she trod,
No arm to stay her, but she leans on God.

While other doublets deviate here and there,
What secret handcuff binds that pretty pair?
Compactest couple! pressing side to side,—
Ah, the white bonnet that reveals the bride!
By the white neckcloth, with its straitened tie
The sober hat, the Sabbath-speaking eye,
Severe and smileless, he that runs may read
The stern disciple of Geneva's creed;
Decent and slow, behold his solemn march;
Silent he enters through yon crowded arch.
A livelier bearing of the outward man,
The light-hued gloves, the undevout ratan,
Now smartly raised or half-profanely twirled,—
A bright, fresh twinkle from the week-day world,—
Tell their plain story;—yes, thine eyes behold
A cheerful Christian from the liberal fold.

Down the chill street that curves in gloomiest shade
What marks betray yon solitary maid?
The cheek's red rose, that speaks of balmier air;
The Celtic blackness of her braided hair;[3]
The gilded missal in her kerchief tied;
Poor Nora, exile from Killarney's side!
Sister in toil, though blanched by colder skies,
That left their azure in her downcast eyes,

See pallid Margaret, Labor's patient child,
Scarce weaned from home, the nursling of the wild
Where white Katahdin o'er the horizon shines,
And broad Penobscot dashes through the pines;
Still, as she hastes, her careful fingers hold
The unfailing hymn-book in its cambric fold.
Six days at drudgery's heavy wheel she stands,
The seventh sweet morning folds her weary hands;
Yes, child of suffering, thou may'st well be sure
He who ordained the Sabbath loves the poor!

This weekly picture faithful memory draws,
Nor claims the noisy tribute of applause;
Faint is the glow such barren hopes can lend,
And frail the line that asks no loftier end.
Trust me, kind listener, I will yet beguile
Thy saddened features of the promised smile;
This magic mantle thou must well divide,
It has its sable and its ermine side;
Yet, ere the lining of the robe appears,
Take thou in silence, what I give in tears.

Dear listening soul, this transitory scene
Of murmuring stillness, busily serene;
This solemn pause, the breathing-space of man,
The halt of toil's exhausted caravan,

Comes sweet with music to thy wearied ear;
Rise with its anthems to a holier sphere!

Deal meekly, gently, with the hopes that guide
The lowliest brother straying from thy side;
If right, they bid thee tremble for thine own,
If wrong, the verdict is for God alone!

What though the champions of thy faith esteem
The sprinkled fountain or baptismal stream;
Shall jealous passions in unseemly strife
Cross their dark weapons o'er the waves of life?

Let my free soul, expanding as it can,
Leave to his scheme the thoughful Puritan;
But Calvin's dogma shall my lips deride?
In that stern faith my angel Mary died;—
Or ask if mercy's milder creed can save,
Sweet sister, risen from thy new-made grave?

True, the harsh founders of thy church reviled
That ancient faith, the trust of Erin's child;
Must thou be raking in the crumbled past
For racks and fagots in her teeth to cast?
See from the ashes of Helvetia's pile
The whitened skull of old Servetus smile!

Round her young heart thy "Romish Upas" threw
Its firm, deep fibres, strengthening as she grew;
Thy sneering voice may call them "Popish tricks," —
Her Latin prayers, her dangling crucifix, —
But *De Profundis* blessed her father's grave;
That "idol" cross her dying mother gave!
  What if some angel looks with equal eyes
On her and thee, the simple and the wise,
Writes each dark fault against thy brighter creed,
And drops a tear with every foolish bead!

  Grieve, as thou must, o'er history's reeking page;
Blush for the wrongs that stain thy happier age;
Strive with the wanderer from the better path,
Bearing thy message meekly, not in wrath;
Weep for the frail that err, the weak that fall,
Have thine own faith, — but hope and pray for all!

  Faith; Conscience; Love. A meaner task remains
And humbler thoughts must creep in lowlier strains;
Shalt thou be honest? Ask the worldly schools,
And all will tell thee knaves are busier fools;
Prudent? Industrious? Let not modern pens
Instruct "Poor Richard's" fellow-citizens.

Be firm! one constant element in luck
Is genuine, solid, old Teutonic pluck;
See yon tall shaft; it felt the earthquake's thrill,
Clung to its base, and greets the sunrise still.

Stick to your aim; the mongrel's hold will slip,
But only crowbars loose the bulldog's grip;
Small as he looks, the jaw that never yields
Drags down the bellowing monarch of the fields!

Yet in opinions look not always back;
Your wake is nothing, mind the coming track;
Leave what you 've done for what you have to do;
Don't be "consistent," but be simply true.

Don't catch the fidgets; you have found your place
Just in the focus of a nervous race,
Fretful to change, and rabid to discuss,
Full of excitements, always in a fuss;—
Think of the patriarchs; then compare as men
These lean-cheeked maniacs of the tongue and pen!
Run, if you like, but try to keep your breath;
Work like a man, but don't be worked to death;
And with new notions,—let me change the rule,—
Don't strike the iron till it 's slightly cool.

Choose well your *set;* our feeble nature seeks
The aid of clubs, the countenance of cliques;
And with this object settle first of all
Your weight of metal and your size of ball.
Track not the steps of such as hold you cheap
Too mean to prize, though good enough to keep;
The "real, genuine, no-mistake Tom Thumbs"
Are little people fed on great men's crumbs.
Yet keep no followers of that hateful brood
That basely mingles with its wholesome food
The tumid reptile, which, the poet said,
Doth wear a precious jewel in his head.

If the wild filly, "Progress," thou would'st ride,
Have young companions ever at thy side;
But, would'st thou stride the staunch old mare, "Success,"
Go with thine elders, though they please thee less.

Shun such as lounge through afternoons and eves,
And on thy dial write "Beware of thieves!"
Felon of minutes, never taught to feel
The worth of treasures which thy fingers steal,
Pick my left pocket of its silver dime,
But spare the right, — it holds my golden time!

Does praise delight thee ? Choose some *ultra* side ;
A sure old recipe, and often tried ;
Be its apostle, congressman, or bard,
Spokesman, or jokesman, only drive it hard ;
But know the forfeit which thy choice abides,
For on two wheels the poor reformer rides,
One black with epithets the *anti* throws,
One white with flattery, painted by the *pros.*

Though books on MANNERS are not out of print,
An honest tongue may drop a harmless hint.
Stop not, unthinking, every friend you meet,
To spin your wordy fabric in the street ;
While you are emptying your colloquial pack,
The fiend *Lumbago* jumps upon his back.
Nor cloud his features with the unwelcome tale
Of how he looks, if haply thin and pale ;
Health is a subject for his child, his wife,
And the rude office that insures his life.
Look in his face, to meet thy neighbor's scu',
Not on his garments, to detect a hole ;
" How to observe," is what thy pages show,
Pride of thy sex, Miss Harriet Martineau !
O, what a precious book the one would be
That taught observers what they 're *not* to see !

I tell in verse,—'t were better done in prose,—
One curious trick that everybody knows;
Once form this habit, and it 's very strange
How long it sticks, how hard it is to change.
Two friendly people, both disposed to smile,
Who meet, like others, every little while,
Instead of passing with a pleasant bow,
And "How d' ye do?" or "How 's your uncle now?"
Impelled by feelings in their nature kind,
But slightly weak, and somewhat undefined,
Rush at each other, make a sudden stand,
Begin to talk, expatiate, and expand;
Each looks quite radiant, seems extremely struck,
Their meeting so was such a piece of luck;
Each thinks the other thinks he 's greatly pleased
To screw the vice in which they both are squeezed;
So there they talk, in dust, or mud, or snow,
Both bored to death, and both afraid to go!
Your hat once lifted, do not hang your fire,
Nor, like slow Ajax, fighting still, retire;
When your old castor on your crown you clap,
Go off; you 've mounted your percussion cap!

Some words on LANGUAGE may be well applied,
And take them kindly, though they touch your pride;

Words lead to things; a scale is more precise,—
Coarse speech, bad grammar, swearing, drinking, vice.
  Our cold Northeaster's icy fetter clips
The native freedom of the Saxon lips;
See the brown peasant of the plastic South,
How all his passions play about his mouth!
With us, the feature that transmits the soul,
A frozen, passive, palsied breathing-hole.
The crampy shackles of the ploughboy's walk
Tie the small muscles when he strives to talk;
Not all the pumice of the polished town
Can smooth this roughness of the barnyard down;
Rich, honored, titled, he betrays his race
By this one mark,—he 's awkward in the face;—
Nature's rude impress, long before he knew
The sunny street that holds the sifted few.
  It can't be helped, though, if we 're taken young,
We gain some freedom of the lips and tongue;
But school and college often try in vain
To break the padlock of our boyhood's chain;
One stubborn word will prove this axiom true;—
No quondam rustic can enunciate *view*.
  A few brief stanzas may be well employed
To speak of errors we can all avoid.

Learning condemns beyond the reach of hope
The careless lips that speak of sŏap for sōap;
Her edict exiles from her fair abode
The clownish voice that utters rŏad for rōad;
Less stern to him who calls his cōat a cŏat,
And steers his bōat, believing it a bŏat,
She pardoned one, our classic city's boast,
Who said at Cambridge, mŏst instead of mōst,
But knit her brows and stamped her angry foot
To hear a Teacher call a rōot a rŏot.
Once more; speak clearly, if you speak at all;
Carve every word before you let it fall;
Don't, like a lecturer or dramatic star,
Try over hard to roll the British R;
Do put your accents in the proper spot;
Don't, — let me beg you, — don't say "How?" for "What?"
And, when you stick on conversation's burs,
Don't strew your pathway with those dreadful *urs*.

From little matters let us pass to less,
And lightly touch the mysteries of DRESS;
The outward forms the inner man reveal, —
We guess the pulp before we cut the peel.

I leave the broadcloth,—coats and all the rest,—
The dangerous waistcoat, called by cockneys "vest,"
The things named "pants" in certain documents,
A word not made for gentlemen, but "gents";
One single precept might the whole condense:
Be sure your tailor is a man of sense;
But add a little care, a decent pride,
And always err upon the sober side.

Three pairs of boots one pair of feet demands,
If polished daily by the owner's hands;
If the dark menial's visit save from this,
Have twice the number, for he 'll sometimes miss.
One pair for critics of the nicer sex,
Close in the instep's clinging circumflex,
Long, narrow, light; the Gallic boot of love,
A kind of cross between a boot and glove.
But, not to tread on everlasting thorns,
And sow in suffering what is reaped in corns,
Compact, but easy, strong, substantial, square,
Let native art compile the medium pair.
The third remains, and let your tasteful skill
Here show some relics of affection still;
Let no stiff cowhide, reeking from the tan,
No rough caoutchouc, no deformed brogan,

Disgrace the tapering outline of your feet,
Though yellow torrents gurgle through the street;
But the *patched* calfskin arm against the flood
In neat, light shoes, impervious to the mud.

Wear seemly gloves; not black, nor yet too light,
And least of all the pair that once was white;
Let the dead party where you told your loves
Bury in peace its dead bouquets and gloves;
Shave like the goat, if so your fancy bids,
But be a parent, — don't neglect your kids.

Have a good hat; the secret of your looks
Lives with the beaver in Canadian brooks;
Virtue may flourish in an old cravat,
But man and nature scorn the shocking hat.
Does beauty slight you from her gay abodes?
Like bright Apollo, you must take to *Rhoades*,
Mount the new castor, — ice itself will melt;
Boots, gloves may fail; the hat is always felt!

Be shy of breast-pins; plain, well-ironed white,
With small pearl buttons, — two of them in sight, —
Is always genuine, while your gems may pass,
Though real diamonds, for ignoble glass;

But spurn those paltry cis-Atlantic lies,
That round his breast the shabby rustic ties;
Breathe not the name, profaned to hallow things
The indignant laundress blushes when she brings!

Our freeborn race, averse to every check,
Has tossed the yoke of Europe from its *neck;*
From the green prairie to the sea-girt town,
The whole wide nation turns its collars down.

The stately neck is manhood's manliest part;
It takes the life-blood freshest from the heart;
With short, curled ringlets close around it spread,
How light and strong it lifts the Grecian head!
Thine, fair Erectheus of Minerva's wall; —
Or thine, young athlete of the Louvre's hall,
Smooth as the pillar flashing in the sun
That filled the arena where thy wreaths were won --
Firm as the band that clasps the antlered spoil
Strained in the winding anaconda's coil!
I spare the contrast; it were only kind
To be a little, nay, intensely blind:
Choose for yourself: I know it cuts your ear;
I know the points will sometimes interfere;

I know that often, like the filial John,
Whom sleep surprised with half his drapery on,
You show your features to the astonished town
With one side standing and the other down; —
But, O my friend! my favorite fellow-man!
If Nature made you on her modern plan,
Sooner than wander with your windpipe bare, —
The fruit of Eden ripening in the air, —
With that lean head-stalk, that protruding chin
Wear standing collars, were they made of tin!
And have a neck-cloth, — by the throat of Jove!
Cut from the funnel of a rusty stove!

The long-drawn lesson narrows to its close,
Chill, slender, slow, the dwindled current flows;
Tired of the ripples on its feeble springs,
Once more the Muse unfolds her upward wings.

Land of my birth, with this unhallowed tongue.
Thy hopes, thy dangers, I perchance had sung;
But who shall sing, in brutal disregard
Of all the essentials of the "native bard"?
Lake, sea, shore, prairie, forest, mountain, fall,
His eye omnivorous must devour them all;

The tallest summits and the broadest tides
His foot must compass with its giant strides,
Where Ocean thunders, where Missouri rolls,
And tread at once the tropics and the poles;
His food all forms of earth, fire, water, air,
His home all space, his birth-place everywhere.

Some grave compatriot, having seen perhaps
The pictured page that goes in Worcester's Maps,
And read in earnest what was said in jest,
"Who drives fat oxen"—please to add the rest,—
Sprung the odd notion that the poet's dreams
Grow in the ratio of his hills and streams;
And hence insisted that the aforesaid "bard,"
Pink of the future,—fancy's pattern-card,—
The babe of nature in the "giant West,"
Must be of course her biggest and her best.

But, were it true that nature's fostering sun
Saves all its daylight for that favorite one,
If for his forehead every wreath she means,
And we, poor children, must not touch the greens;
Since rocks and rivers cannot take the road
To seek the elected in his own abode,

Some voice must answer, for her precious heir,
One solemn question;—Who shall pay his fare?

O when at length the expected bard shall come,
Land of our pride, to strike thine echoes dumb,
(And many a voice exclaims in prose and rhyme
It 's getting late, and he 's behind his time,)
When all thy mountains clap their hands in joy,
And all thy cataracts thunder "That 's the boy,"—
Say if with him the reign of song shall end,
And Heaven declare its final dividend?

Be calm, dear brother! whose impassioned strain
Comes from an alley watered by a drain;
The little Mincio, dribbling to the Po,
Beats all the epics of the Hoang Ho;
If loved in earnest by the tuneful maid,
Don't mind their nonsense,—never be afraid!

The nurse of poets feeds her winged brood
By common firesides, on familiar food;
In a low hamlet, by a narrow stream,
Where bovine rustics used to doze and dream,
She filled young William's fiery fancy full,
While old John Shakspeare talked of beeves and wool!

No Alpine needle, with its climbing spire,
Brings down for mortals the Promethean fire,
If careless nature have forgot to frame
An altar worthy of the sacred flame.
Unblest by any save the goat-herd's lines,
Mont Blanc rose soaring through his "sea of pines";
In vain the Arve and Arveiron dash,
No hymn salutes them but the Ranz des Vaches,
Till lazy Coleridge, by the morning's light,
Gazed for a moment on the fields of white,
And lo, the glaciers found at length a tongue,
Mont Blanc was vocal, and Chamouni sung!

Children of wealth or want, to each is given
One spot of green, and all the blue of heaven!
Enough, if these their outward shows impart;
The rest is thine, — the scenery of the heart.
If passion's hectic in thy stanzas glow,
Thy heart's best life-blood ebbing as they flow,
If with thy verse thy strength and bloom distil,
Drained by the pulses of the fevered thrill;
If sound's sweet effluence polarize thy brain,
And thoughts turn crystals in thy fluid strain, —
Nor rolling ocean, nor the prairie's bloom,
Nor streaming cliffs, nor rayless cavern's gloom,

Need'st thou, young poet, to inform thy line;
Thy own broad signet stamps thy song divine!
  Let others gaze where silvery streams are rolled,
And chase the rainbow for its cup of gold;
To thee all landscapes wear a heavenly dye,
Changed in the glance of thy prismatic eye;
Nature evoked thee in sublimer throes,
For thee her inmost Arethusa flows, —
The mighty mother's living depths are stirred, —
Thou art the starred Osiris of the herd!

  A few brief lines; they touch on solemn chords,
And hearts may leap to hear their honest words;
Yet, ere the jarring bugle-blast is blown,
The softer lyre shall breathe its soothing tone.

  New England! proudly may thy children claim
Their honored birthright by its humblest name!
Cold are thy skies, but, ever fresh and clear,
No rank malaria stains thine atmosphere;
No fungous weeds invade thy scanty soil,
Scarred by the ploughshares of unslumbering toil.
Long may the doctrines by thy sages taught,
Raised from the quarries where their sires have wrought.

Be like the granite of thy rock-ribbed land,—
As slow to rear, as obdurate to stand;
And as the ice, that leaves thy crystal mine,
Chills the fierce alcohol in the Creole's wine,
So may the doctrines of thy sober school
Keep the hot theories of thy neighbours cool!

If ever, trampling on her ancient path,
Cankered by treachery, or inflamed by wrath,
With smooth "Resolves," or with discordant cries,
The mad Briareus of disunion rise,
Chiefs of New England! by your sires' renown,
Dash the red torches of the rebel down!
Flood his black hearth-stone till its flames expire,
Though your old Sachem fanned his council-fire!

But if at last,—her fading cycle run,—
The tongue must forfeit what the arm has won,
Then rise, wild Ocean! roll thy surging shock
Full on old Plymouth's desecrated rock!
Scale the proud shaft degenerate hands have hewn,
Where bleeding Valor stained the flowers of June!
Sweep in one tide her spires and turrets down,
And howl her dirge above Monadnock's crown!

List not the tale; the Pilgrim's hallowed shore,
Though strewn with weeds, is granite at the core;
O rather trust that He who made her free
Will keep her true, as long as faith shall be!

Farewell! yet lingering through the destined hour,
Leave, sweet Enchantress, one memorial flower!

An Angel, floating o'er the waste of snow
That clad our western desert, long ago,
(The same fair spirit, who, unseen by day,
Shone as a star along the Mayflower's way,)
Sent, the first herald of the Heavenly plan,
To choose on earth a resting-place for man, —
Tired with his flight along the unvaried field,
Turned to soar upwards, when his glance revealed
A calm, bright bay, enclosed in rocky bounds,
And at its entrance stood three sister mounds.

The Angel spake: "This threefold hill shall be
The home of Arts, the nurse of Liberty!
One stately summit from its shaft shall pour
Its deep-red blaze, along the darkened shore;
Emblem of thoughts, that, kindling far and wide,
In danger's night shall be a nation's guide.

One swelling crest the citadel shall crown,
Its slanted bastions black with battle's frown,
And bid the sons that tread its scowling heights
Bare their strong arms for man and all his rights!
One silent steep along the northern wave
Shall hold the patriarch's and the hero's grave;
When fades the torch, when o'er the peaceful scene
The embattled fortress smiles in living green,
The cross of Faith, the anchor staff of Hope,
Shall stand eternal on its grassy slope;
There through all time shall faithful Memory tell:
"Here Virtue toiled, and Patriot Valor fell;
Thy free, proud fathers slumber at thy side,
Live as they lived, or perish as they died!"

NOTES.

Note 1. Page 197.

Οἵη περ φύλλων γενεὴ, τοιῇδε καὶ ἀνδρῶν. — *Iliad*, VI., 146.

Wesley quotes this line in his account of his early doubts and perplexities. See *Southey's Life of Wesley*, Vol. II., p. 185.

Note 2. Page 203.

The churches referred to in the lines which follow are

1. "King's Chapel," the foundation of which was laid by Governor Shirley in 1749.

2. The church in Brattle Square, consecrated in 1773. The completion of this edifice, the design of which included a spire, was prevented by the troubles of the Revolution, and its plain square tower presents nothing more attractive than a massive simplicity. In the front of this tower is still seen, half imbedded in the brick-work, a cannon-ball, which was thrown from the American fortifications at Cambridge, during the bombardment of the city, then occupied by the British troops.

3. The "Old South," first occupied for public worship in 1730.

4. Park Street Church, built in 1809, the tall, white steeple of which is the most conspicuous of all the Boston spires.

5. Christ Church, opened for public worship in 1723, and containing a set of eight bells, the only chime in Boston.

Note 3. Page 206.

For the propriety of the term "*Celtic* blackness," see *Lawrence's Lectures*, (Salem, 1828,) pp. 452, 453. But the ancient Celts appear to have been a xanthous, or fair-haired race. See *Prichard's Nat. Hist. of Man*, (London, 1843,) pp. 183, 193, 196.

Note 4. Page 225.

The name first given by the English to Boston was TRI-MOUNTAIN. The three hills upon and around which the city is built are Beacon Hill, Fort Hill, and Copp's Hill.

In the early records of the Colony, it is mentioned, under date of May 6th, 1635, that "A BEACON is to be set on the Sentry hill, at Boston, to give notice to the country of any danger; to be guarded by one man stationed near, and fired as occasion may be." The last Beacon was blown down in 1789.

The eastern side of Fort Hill was formerly "a ragged cliff, that seemed placed by nature in front of the entrance to the harbor for the purposes of defence, to which it was very soon applied, and from which it obtained its present name." Its summit is now a beautiful green enclosure.

Copp's Hill was used as a burial-ground from a very early period. The part of it employed for this purpose slopes towards the water upon the northern side. From its many interesting records of the dead I select the following, which may serve to show what kind of dust it holds.

"Here lies buried in a
Stone Grave 10 feet deep,
Cap[t] DANIEL MALCOLM Merch[t]
who departed this Life
October 23d, 1769,
Aged 44 years,
a true son of Liberty,
a Friend to the Publick,
an Enemy to oppression,
and one of the foremost
in opposing the Revenue Acts
on America."

The gravestone from which I copied this inscription is bruised and splintered by the bullets of the British soldiers.

THE PILGRIM'S VISION.

In the hour of twilight shadows
    The Puritan looked out;
He thought of the "bloudy Salvages"
    That lurked all round about,
Of Wituwamet's pictured knife
    And Pecksuot's whooping shout;
For the baby's limbs were feeble,
    Though his father's arms were stout

His home was a freezing cabin
    Too bare for the hungry rat,
Its roof was thatched with ragged grass
    And bald enough of that;
The hole that served for casement
    Was glazed with an ancient hat;
And the ice was gently thawing
    From the log whereon he sat.

Along the dreary landscape
His eyes went to and fro,
The trees all clad in icicles,
The streams that did not flow;
A sudden thought flashed o'er him,—
A dream of long ago,—
He smote his leathern jerkin
And murmured "Even so!"

"Come hither, God-be-Glorified,
And sit upon my knee,
Behold the dream unfolding,
Whereof I spake to thee
By the winter's hearth in Leyden
And on the stormy sea;
True is the dream's beginning,—
So may its ending be!

"I saw in the naked forest
Our scattered remnant cast,
A screen of shivering branches
Between them and the blast;
The snow was falling round them,
The dying fell as fast;
I looked to see them perish,
When lo, the vision passed.

"Again mine eyes were opened; —
The feeble had waxed strong,
The babes had grown to sturdy men,
The remnant was a throng;
By shadowed lake and winding stream
And all the shores along,
The howling demons quaked to hear
The Christian's godly song.

"They slept, — the village fathers, —
By river, lake and shore,
When far adown the steep of Time
The vision rose once more;
I saw along the winter snow
A spectral column pour,
And high above their broken ranks
A tattered flag they bore.

"Their Leader rode before them,
Of bearing calm and high,
The light of Heaven's own kindling
Throned in his awful eye;
These were a Nation's champions
Her dread appeal to try;
God for the right! I faltered,
And lo, the train passed by.

"Once more;—the strife is ended,
The solemn issue tried,
The Lord of Hosts, his mighty arm
Has helped our Israel's side;
Gray stone and grassy hillock
Tell where our martyrs died,
But peaceful smiles the harvest,
And stainless flows the tide.

"A crash,—as when some swollen cloud
Cracks o'er the tangled trees!
With side to side, and spar to spar,
Whose smoking decks are these?
I know Saint George's blood-red cross,
Thou Mistress of the Seas,—
But what is she, whose streaming bars
Roll out before the breeze?

"Ah, well her iron ribs are knit,
Whose thunders strive to quell
The bellowing throats, the blazing lips,
That pealed the Armada's knell!
The mist was cleared,—a wreath of stars
Rose o'er the crimsoned swell,
And, wavering from its haughty peak,
The cross of England fell!

"O trembling Faith! though dark the morn,
A heavenly torch is thine;
While feebler races melt away,
And paler orbs decline,
Still shall the fiery pillar's ray
Along thy pathway shine,
To light the chosen tribe that sought
This Western Palestine!

"I see the living tide roll on;
It crowns with flaming towers
The icy capes of Labrador,
The Spaniard's 'land of flowers'!
It streams beyond the splintered ridge
That parts the Northern showers;
From eastern rock to sunset wave
The Continent is ours!"

He ceased,—the grim old Puritan,—
Then softly bent to cheer
The pilgrim-child, whose wasting face
Was meekly turned to hear;
And drew his toil-worn sleeve across,
To brush the manly tear
From cheeks that never changed in woe,
And never blanched in fear.

The weary pilgrim slumbers,
  His resting-place unknown;
His hands were crossed, his lids were closed,
  The dust was o'er him strown;
The drifting soil, the mouldering leaf,
  Along the sod were blown;
His mound has melted into earth,
  His memory lives alone.

So let it live unfading,
  The memory of the dead,
Long as the pale anemone
  Springs where their tears were shed,
Or, raining in the summer's wind
  In flakes of burning red,
The wild rose sprinkles with its leaves
  The turf where once they bled!

Yea, when the frowning bulwarks
  That guard this holy strand
Have sunk beneath the trampling surge
  In beds of sparkling sand,
While in the waste of ocean
  One hoary rock shall stand,
Be this its latest legend,—
  HERE WAS THE PILGRIM'S LAND!

A MODEST REQUEST.

COMPLIED WITH AFTER THE DINNER AT PRESIDENT EVERETT'S INAUGURATION.

Scene, — a back parlour in a certain square,
Or court, or lane,— in short no matter where;
Time,— early morning, dear to simple souls
Who love its sunshine, and its fresh-baked rolls;
Persons, — take pity on this telltale blush,
That, like the Æthiop, whispers "Hush, O hush!"

Delightful scene! where smiling comfort broods,
Nor business frets, nor anxious care intrudes;
O si sic omnia! were it ever so!
But what is stable in this world below!
Medio e fonte,— Virtue has her faults,—
The clearest fountains taste of Epsom salts;
We snatch the cup and lift to drain it dry,—
Its central dimple holds a drowning fly!

Strong is the pine by Maine's ambrosial streams,
But stronger augers pierce its thickest beams;
No iron gate, no spiked and pannelled door,
Can keep out death, the postman, or the bore;—
O for a world where peace and silence reign,
And blunted dulness terebrates in vain!
—The door bell jingles,—enter Richard Fox,
And takes this letter from his leathern box.

"Dear Sir,
In writing on a former day,
One little matter I forgot to say;
I now inform you in a single line,
On Thursday next our purpose is to *dine.*
The act of feeding, as you understand,
Is but a fraction of the work in hand;
Its nobler half is that ethereal meat
The papers call 'the intellectual treat';
Songs, speeches, toasts, around the festive board,
Drowned in the juice the College pumps afford;
For only water flanks our knives and forks,
So, sink or float, we swim without the corks.
Yours is the art, by native genius taught,
To clothe in eloquence the naked thought;

Yours is the skill its music to prolong
Through the sweet effluence of mellifluous song;
Yours the quaint trick to cram the pithy line
That cracks so crisply over bubbling wine;
And since success your various gifts attends,
We,—that is I and all your numerous friends,—
Expect from you,—your single self a host,—
A speech, a song, excuse me, *and* a toast;
Nay, not to haggle on so small a claim,
A few of each, or several of the same.
(Signed) Yours, *most truly*, ——— "

No! my sight must fail,—
If that ain't Judas on the largest scale!

Well, this *is* modest;—nothing else than that?
My coat? my boots? my pantaloons? my hat?
My stick? my gloves? as well as all my wits,
Learning and linen,—everything that fits!

Jack, said my lady, is it grog you'll try,
Or punch, or toddy, if perhaps you're dry?
Ah, said the sailor, though I can't refuse,
You know, my lady, 't ain't for me to choose;—

I 'll take the grog to finish off my lunch,
And drink the toddy while you mix the punch.

THE SPEECH. (The speaker, rising to be seen,
Looks very red, because so very green.)
I rise — I rise — with unaffected fear,
(Louder!—speak louder!—who the deuce can hear ?)
I rise — I said — with undisguised dismay —
— Such are my feelings as I rise, I say !
Quite unprepared to face this learned throng,
Already gorged with eloquence and song;
Around my view are ranged on either hand
The genius, wisdom, virtue of the land;
" Hands that the rod of empire might have swayed "
Close at my elbow stir their lemonade;
Would you like Homer learn to write and speak,
That bench is groaning with its weight of Greek;
Behold the naturalist that in his teens
Found six new species in a dish of greens;
And lo, the master in a statelier walk,
Whose annual ciphering takes a ton of chalk;
And there the linguist, that by common roots
Through all their nurseries tracks old Noah's shoots,—

How Shem's proud children reared the Assyrian piles,
While Ham's were scattered through the Sandwich
Isles!

— Fired at the thought of all the present shows,
My kindling fancy down the future flows;
I see the glory of the coming days
O'er Time's horizon shoot its streaming rays;
Near and more near the radiant morning draws
In living lustre (rapturous applause);
From east to west the blazing heralds run,
Loosed from the chariot of the ascending sun,
Through the long vista of uncounted years
In cloudless splendor (three tremendous cheers).
My eye prophetic, as the depths unfold,
Sees a new advent of the age of gold;
While o'er the scene new generations press,
New heroes rise the coming time to bless,—
Not such as Homer's, who, we read in Pope,
Dined without forks and never heard of soap,—
Not such as May to Marlborough Chapel brings,
Lean, hungry, savage, anti-everythings,
Copies of Luther in the pasteboard style,—
But genuine articles,— the true Carlyle;

While far on high the blazing orb shall shed
Its central light on Harvard's holy head,
And Learning's ensigns ever float unfurled
Here in the focus of the new-born world!

The speaker stops, and, trampling down the pause,
Roars through the hall the thunder of applause,
One stormy gust of long suspended Ahs!
One whirlwind chaos of insane hurrahs!

THE SONG. But this demands a briefer line,—
A shorter muse, and not the old long Nine;—
Long metre answers for a common song,
Though common metre does not answer long

She came beneath the forest dome
  To seek its peaceful shade,
An exile from her ancient home,—
  A poor forsaken maid;
No banner, flaunting high above,
  No blazoned cross, she bore;
One holy book of light and love
  Was all her worldly store.

The dark brown shadows passed away,
And wider spread the green,
And, where the savage used to stray,
The rising mart was seen;
So, when the laden winds had brought
Their showers of golden rain,
Her lap some precious gleanings caught,
Like Ruth's amid the grain.

But wrath soon gathered uncontrolled
Among the baser churls,
To see her ancles red with gold,
Her forehead white with pearls;
"Who gave to thee the glittering bands
That lace thine azure veins?
Who bade thee lift those snow-white hands
We bound in gilded chains?"

These are the gems my children gave,
The stately dame replied;
The wise, the gentle, and the brave,
I nurtured at my side;
If envy still your bosom stings,
Take back their rims of gold;
My sons will melt their wedding rings,
And give a hundred fold!

THE TOAST. — O tell me, ye who thoughtless ask
Exhausted nature for a threefold task,
In wit or pathos if one share remains,
A safe investment for an ounce of brains?
Hard is the job to launch the desperate pun,
A pun-job dangerous as the Indian one.
Turned by the current of some stronger wit
Back from the object that you mean to hit,
Like the strange missile which the Australian throws
Your verbal *boomerang* slaps you on the nose.
One vague inflection spoils the whole with doubt,
One trivial letter ruins all, left out;
A knot can choke a felon into clay,
A not will save him, spelt without the k;
The smallest word has some unguarded spot,
And danger lurks in i without a dot.

Thus great Achilles, who had shown his zeal
In healing wounds, died of a wounded heel;
Unhappy chief, who, when in childhood doused,
Had saved his bacon, had his feet been soused!
Accursed heel that killed a hero stout!
O, had your mother known that you were out,
Death had not entered at the trifling part
That still defies the small chirurgeon's art

With corns and bunions,—not the glorious John
Who wrote the book we all have pondered on,—
But other bunions, bound in fleecy hose,
To "Pilgrim's Progress" unrelenting foes!

A health, unmingled with the reveller's wine,
To him whose title is indeed divine;
Truth's sleepless watchman on her midnight tower,
Whose lamp burns brightest when the tempests lower.
O who can tell with what a leaden flight
Drag the long watches of his weary night;
While at his feet the hoarse and blinding gale
Strews the torn wreck and bursts the fragile sail,
When stars have faded, when the wave is dark,
When rocks and sands embrace the foundering bark,
And still he pleads with unavailing cry,
Behold the light, O wanderer, look or die!

A health, fair Themis! Would the enchanted vine
Wreathed its green tendrils round this cup of thine;
If Learning's radiance fill thy modern court,
Its glorious sunshine streams through Blackstone's port!

Lawyers are thirsty, and their clients too,
Witness at least, if memory serve me true,
Those old tribunals, famed for dusty suits,
Where men sought justice ere they brushed their boots;—
And what can match, to solve a learned doubt,
The warmth within that comes from "cold without"?

Health to the art whose glory is to give
The crowning boon that makes it life to live.
Ask not her home;—the rock where nature flings
Her arctic lichen, last of living things,
The gardens, fragrant with the orient's balm,
From the low jasmine to the star-like palm,
Hail her as mistress o'er the distant waves,
And yield their tribute to her wandering slaves.
Wherever, moistening the ungrateful soil,
The tear of suffering tracks the path of toil,
There, in the anguish of his fevered hours,
Her gracious finger points to healing flowers;
Where the lost felon steals away to die,
Her soft hand waves before his closing eye;
Where hunted misery finds his darkest lair,
The midnight taper shows her kneeling there!

VIRTUE,—the guide that men and nations own;
And LAW,—the bulwark that protects her throne;
And HEALTH,—to all its happiest charm that lends;
These and their servants, man's untiring friends;
Pour the bright lymph that Heaven itself lets fall,—
In one fair bumper let us toast them all!

NUX POSTCŒNATICA.

I WAS sitting with my microscope, upon my parlour rug,
With a very heavy quarto and a very lively bug;
The true bug had been organized with only two antennæ,
But the humbug in the copperplate would have them twice as many.

And I thought, like Dr. Faustus, of the emptiness of art,
How we take a fragment for the whole, and call the whole a part,
When I heard a heavy footstep that was loud enough for two,
And a man of forty entered, exclaiming,—"How d'ye do?"

He was not a ghost, my visitor, but solid flesh and
bone;
He wore a Palo Alto hat, his weight was twenty
stone;
(It 's odd how hats expand their brims as riper years
invade,
As if when life had reached its noon, it wanted them
for shade!)

I lost my focus,—dropped my book,—the bug, who
was a flea,
At once exploded, and commenced experiments on
me.
They have a certain heartiness that frequently appals,—
Those mediæval gentlemen in semilunar smalls!

"My boy," he said—(colloquial ways,—the vast,
broad-hatted man,)
"Come dine with us on Thursday next,—you must,
you know you can;
We 're going to have a roaring time, with lots of fun
and noise,
Distinguished guests, et cetera, the JUDGE, and all the
boys."

Not so, — I said, — my temporal bones are showing pretty clear
It 's time to stop,—just look and see that hair above this ear;
My golden days are more than spent,—and, what is very strange,
If these are real silver hairs, I 'm getting lots of change.

Besides — my prospects — don't you know that people won't employ
A man that wrongs his manliness by laughing like a boy?
And suspect the azure blossom that unfolds upon a shoot,
As if wisdom's old potato could not flourish at its root!

It 's a very fine reflection, when you 're etching out a smile
On a copper plate of faces that would stretch at least a mile,
That, what with sneers from enemies, and cheapening shrugs of friends,
It will cost you all the earnings that a month of labor lends!

It 's a vastly pleasing prospect, when you 're screwing
out a laugh,
That your very next year's income is diminished by a
half,
And a little boy trips barefoot that Pegasus may go,
And the baby's milk is watered that your Helicon may
flow!

No;—the joke has been a good one,—but I 'm getting
fond of quiet,
And I don't like deviations from my customary diet;
So I think I will not go with you to hear the toasts and
speeches,
But stick to old Montgomery Place, and have some pig
and peaches.

The fat man answered: — Shut your mouth, and hear
the genuine creed;
The true essentials of a feast are only fun and feed;
The force that wheels the planets round delights in
spinning tops,
And that young earthquake t' other day was great at
shaking props.

I tell you what, philosopher, if all the longest heads
That ever knocked their sinciputs in stretching on their beds
Were round one great mahogany, I 'd beat those fine old folks
With twenty dishes, twenty fools, and twenty clever jokes!

Why, if Columbus should be there, the company would beg
He 'd show that little trick of his of balancing the egg!
Milton to Stilton would give in, and Solomon to Salmon,
And Roger Bacon be a bore, and Francis Bacon gammon!

And as for all the "patronage" of all the clowns and boors
That squint their little narrow eyes at any freak of yours,
Do leave them to your prosier friends,— such fellows ought to die
When rhubarb is so very scarce and ipecac so high!

And so I come,— like Lochinvar, to tread a single
measure,
To purchase with a loaf of bread a sugar-plum of
pleasure,
To enter for the cup of glass that 's run for after dinner,
Which yields a single sparkling draught, then breaks
and cuts the winner.

Ah, that 's the way delusion comes,—a glass of old
Madeira,
A pair of visual diaphragms revolved by Jane or
Sarah,
And down go vows and promises without the slightest
question
If eating words won't compromise the organs of
digestion!

And yet, among my native shades, beside my nursing
mother,
Where every stranger seems a friend, and every friend
a brother,
I feel the old convivial glow (unaided) o'er me stealing,--
The warm, champagny, old-particular, brandy-punchy
feeling.

We 're all alike;—Vesuvius flings the scoriæ from his
fountain,
But down they come in volleying rain back to the
burning mountain;
We leave, like those volcanic stones, our precious Alma
Mater,
But will keep dropping in again to see the dear old
crater.

ON LENDING A PUNCH-BOWL.

This ancient silver bowl of mine,—it tells of good old times,
Of joyous days, and jolly nights, and merry Christmas chimes;
They were a free and jovial race, but honest, brave, and true,
That dipped their ladle in the punch when this old bowl was new.

A Spanish galleon brought the bar,—so runs the ancient tale;
'T was hammered by an Antwerp smith, whose arm was like a flail;
And now and then between the strokes, for fear his strength should fail,
He wiped his brow, and quaffed a cup of good old Flemish ale.

'T was purchased by an English squire to please his loving dame,
Who saw the cherubs, and conceived a longing for the same;
And oft, as on the ancient stock another twig was found,
'T was filled with caudle spiced and hot, and handed smoking round.

But, changing hands, it reached at length a Puritan divine,
Who used to follow Timothy, and take a little wine,
But hated punch and prelacy; and so it was, perhaps,
He went to Leyden, where he found conventicles and schnaps.

And then, of course, you know what 's next,— it left the Dutchman's shore
With those that in the Mayflower came,— a hundred souls and more,—
Along with all the furniture, to fill their new abodes,—
To judge by what is still on hand, at least a hundred loads.

'T was on a dreary winter's eve, the night was closing dim,
When old Miles Standish took the bowl, and filled it to the brim;
The little Captain stood and stirred the posset with his sword,
And all his sturdy men at arms were ranged about the the board.

He poured the fiery Hollands in,— the man that never feared,—
He took a long and solemn draught, and wiped his yellow beard;
And one by one the musketeers,— the men that fought and prayed,—
All drank as 't were their mother's milk, and not a man afraid.

That night, affrighted from his nest, the screaming eagle flew,
He heard the Pequot's ringing whoop, the soldier's wild halloo;
And there the sachem learned the rule he taught to kitn and kin,
"Run from the white man when you find he smells of Hollands gin!"

A hundred years, and fifty more, had spread their leaves and snows,
A thousand rubs had flattened down each little cherub's nose;
When once again the bowl was filled, but not in mirth or joy,
'T was mingled by a mother's hand to cheer her parting boy.

Drink, John, she said, 't will do you good,—poor child, you 'll never bear
This working in the dismal trench, out in the midnight air;
And if,—God bless me,—you were hurt, 't would keep away the chill;
So John *did* drink,—and well he wrought that night at Bunker's Hill!

I tell you, there was generous warmth in good old English cheer;
I tell you, 't was a pleasant thought to bring its symbol here.
'T is but the fool that loves excess;—hast thou a drunken soul?
Thy bane is in thy shallow skull, not in my silver bowl!

I love the memory of the past,—its pressed yet fragrant flowers,—
The moss that clothes its broken walls,—the ivy on its towers,—
Nay, this poor bauble it bequeathed,—my eyes grow moist and dim,
To think of all the vanished joys that danced around its brim.

Then fill a fair and honest cup, and bear it straight to me;
The goblet hallows all it holds, whate'er the liquid be;
And may the cherubs on its face protect me from the sin,
That dooms one to those dreadful words,—"My dear, where *have* you been?"

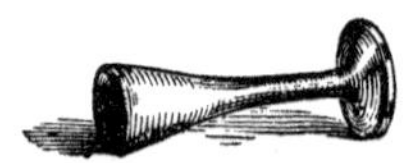

THE STETHOSCOPE SONG.

A PROFESSIONAL BALLAD.

THERE was a young man in Boston town
He bought him a STETHOSCOPE nice and new,
All mounted and finished and polished down,
With an ivory cap and a stopper too.

It happened a spider within did crawl,
And spun him a web of ample size,
Wherein there chanced one day to fall
A couple of very imprudent flies.

The first was a bottle-fly, big and blue,
    The second was smaller, and thin and long;
So there was a concert between the two,
    Like an octave flute and a tavern gong.

Now being from Paris but recently,
    This fine young man would show his skill;
And so they gave him, his hand to try,
    A hospital patient extremely ill.

Some said that his *liver* was short of *bile*,
    And some that his *heart* was over size,
While some kept arguing all the while
    He was crammed with *tubercles* up to his eyes.

This fine young man then up stepped he,
    And all the doctors made a pause;
Said he,—The man must die, you see,
    By the fifty-seventh of Louis's laws.

But, since the case is a desperate one,
    To explore his chest it may be well;
For, if he should die and it were not done,
    You know the *autopsy* would not tell.

Then out his stethoscope he took,
    And on it placed his curious ear;
Mon Dieu! said he, with a knowing look,
    Why here is a sound that 's mighty queer!

The *bourdonnement* is very clear,—
    Amphoric buzzing, as I 'm alive!
Five doctors took their turn to hear;
    Amphoric buzzing, said all the five.

There 's *empyema* beyond a doubt;
    We 'll plunge a *trocar* in his side.—
The diagnosis was made out,
    They tapped the patient; so he died.

Now such as hate new-fashioned toys
    Began to look extremely glum;
They said that *rattles* were made for boys,
    And vowed that his *buzzing* was all a hum.

There was an old lady had long been sick,
    And what was the matter none did know;
Her pulse was slow, though her tongue was quick;
    To her this knowing youth must go.

So there the nice old lady sat,
    With phials and boxes all in a row;
She asked the young doctor what he was at,
    To thump her and tumble her ruffles so.

Now, when the stethoscope came out,
    The flies began to buzz and whiz;—
O ho! the matter is clear, no doubt;
    An *aneurism* there plainly is.

The *bruit de râpe* and the *bruit de scie*
    And the *bruit de diable* are all combined;
How happy Bouillaud would be,
    If he a case like this could find!

Now, when the neighbouring doctors found
    A case so rare had been descried,
They every day her ribs did pound
    In squads of twenty; so she died.

Then six young damsels, slight and frail,
    Received this kind young doctor's cares;
They all were getting slim and pale,
    And short of breath on mounting stairs.

They all made rhymes with "sighs" and "skies,"
And loathed their puddings and buttered rolls,
And dieted, much to their friends' surprise,
On pickles and pencils and chalk and coals.

So fast their little hearts did bound,
The frightened insects buzzed the more;
So over all their chests he found
The *râle sifflant*, and *râle sonore*.

He shook his head;—there 's grave disease,—
I greatly fear you all must die;
A slight *post-mortem*, if you please,
Surviving friends would gratify.

The six young damsels wept aloud,
Which so prevailed on six young men,
That each his honest love avowed,
Whereat they all got well again.

This poor young man was all aghast;
The price of stethoscopes came down;
And so he was reduced at last
To practise in a country town.

The doctors being very sore,
  A stethoscope they did devise,
That had a rammer to clear the bore,
  With a knob at the end to kill the flies.

Now use your ears, all you that can,
  But don't forget to mind your eyes,
Or you may be cheated, like this young man,
  By a couple of silly, abnormal flies.

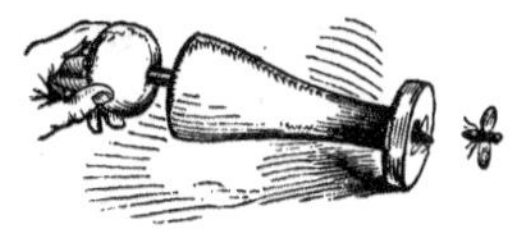

EXTRACTS FROM A MEDICAL POEM.

THE STABILITY OF SCIENCE.

THE feeble seabirds, blinded in the storms,
On some tall lighthouse dash their little forms,
And the rude granite scatters for their pains
Those small deposits that were meant for brains.
Yet the proud fabric in the morning's sun
Stands all unconscious of the mischief done;
Still the red beacon pours its evening rays
For the lost pilot with as full a blaze,
Nay, shines, all radiance, o'er the scattered fleet
Of gulls and boobies brainless at its feet.
I tell their fate, though courtesy disclaims
To call our kind by such ungentle names;
Yet, if your rashness bid you vainly dare,
Think of their doom, ye simple, and beware!

See where aloft its hoary forehead rears
The towering pride of twice a thousand years!
Far, far below the vast incumbent pile
Sleeps the gray rock from art's Ægean isle;
Its massive courses, circling as they rise,
Swell from the waves to mingle with the skies;
There every quarry lends its marble spoil,
And clustering ages blend their common toil;
The Greek, the Roman, reared its ancient walls,
The silent Arab arched its mystic halls;
In that fair niche, by countless billows laved,
Trace the deep lines that Sydenham engraved;
On yon broad front that breasts the changing swell,
Mark where the ponderous sledge of Hunter fell,
By that square buttress look where Louis stands,
The stone yet warm from his uplifted hands;
And say, O Science, shall thy life-blood freeze
When fluttering folly flaps on walls like these?

A PORTRAIT.

SIMPLE in youth, but not austere in age;
Calm, but not cold, and cheerful though a sage;
Too true to flatter, and too kind to sneer,
And only just when seemingly severe;

So gently blending courtesy and art,
That wisdom's lips seemed borrowing friendship's heart;
Taught by the sorrows that his age had known
In others' trials to forget his own,
As hour by hour his lengthened day declined,
The sweeter radiance lingered o'er his mind.
Cold were the lips that spoke his early praise,
And hushed the voices of his morning days,
Yet the same accents dwelt on every tongue,
And love renewing kept him ever young.

A SENTIMENT.

'*Ο βιος βραχυς*— life is but a song —
'*Η τεχνη μακρη* — art is wondrous long;
Yet to the wise her paths are ever fair,
And Patience smiles, though Genius may despair.
Give us but knowledge, though by slow degrees,
And blend our toil with moments bright as these;
Let Friendship's accents cheer our doubtful way,
And Love's pure planet lend its guiding ray, —
Our tardy Art shall wear an angel's wings,
And life shall lengthen with the joy it brings!

A SONG OF OTHER DAYS.

As o'er the glacier's frozen sheet
Breathes soft the Alpine rose,
So, through life's desert springing sweet,
The flower of friendship grows;
And as, where'er the roses grow,
Some rain or dew descends,
'T is nature's law that wine should flow
To wet the lips of friends.

Then once again, before we part,
My empty glass shall ring;
And he that has the warmest heart
Shall loudest laugh and sing.

They say we were not born to eat;
  But gray-haired sages think
It means,—Be moderate in your meat
  And partly live to drink;
For baser tribes the rivers flow
  That know not wine or song,
Man wants but little drink below,
  But wants that little strong.

Then once again, etc.

If one bright drop is like the gem
  That decks a monarch's crown,
One goblet holds a diadem
  Of rubies melted down!
A fig for Cæsar's blazing brow,
  But, like the Egyptian queen,
Bid each dissolving jewel glow
  My thirsty lips between.

Then once again, etc.

The Grecian's mound, the Roman's urn,
  Are silent when we call,
Yet still the purple grapes return
  To cluster on the wall;

It was a bright Immortal's head
    They circled with the vine,
And o'er their best and bravest dead
    They poured the dark-red wine.

Then once again, etc.

Methinks o'er every sparkling glass
    Young Eros waves his wings,
And echoes o'er its dimples pass
    From dead Anacreon's strings;
And, tossing round its beaded brim
    Their locks of floating gold,
With bacchant dance and choral hymn
    Return the nymphs of old.

Then once again, etc.

A welcome then to joy and mirth,
    From hearts as fresh as ours,
To scatter o'er the dust of earth
    Their sweetly mingled flowers;

T' is Wisdom's self the cup that fills
In spite of Folly's frown,
And Nature, from her vine-clad hills,
That rains her life-blood down!

Then once again, etc.

A SENTIMENT.

The pledge of Friendship! it is still divine,
Though watery floods have quenched its burning wine;
Whatever vase the sacred drops may hold,
The gourd, the shell, the cup of beaten gold,
Around its brim the hand of Nature throws
A garland sweeter than the banquet's rose.
Bright are the blushes of the vine-wreathed bowl,
Warm with the sunshine of Anacreon's soul,
But dearer memories gild the tasteless wave
That fainting Sidney perished as he gave.
'T is the heart's current lends the cup its glow,
Whate'er the fountain whence the draught may flow,—
The diamond dew-drops sparkling through the sand,
Scooped by the Arab in his sunburnt hand,
Or the dark streamlet oozing from the snow,
Where creep and crouch the shuddering Esquimaux,—

Ay, in the stream that ere again we meet,
Shall burst the pavement, glistening at our feet,
And, stealing silent from its leafy hills,
Thread all our alleys with its thousand rills, —
In each pale draught if generous feeling blend,
And o'er the goblet friend shall smile on friend,
Even cold Cochituate every heart shall warm,
And genial Nature still defy reform!

www.ingramcontent.com/pod-product-compliance
Lightning Source LLC
LaVergne TN
LVHW010210110826
845151LV00004B/1046

* 9 7 8 1 4 2 5 5 2 9 1 0 9 *